THE FUR TRADE
IN CANADA

Michael Payne

JAMES LORIMER & COMPANY LTD., PUBLISHERS

TORONTO

James Lorimer & Company Ltd. acknowledges the support of the Department of Canadian Heritage and the
Ontario Arts Council in the development of writing
and publishing in Canada.

We acknowledge the support of the Government of
Ontario through the Ontario Media Development
Corporation's Ontario Book Initiative. We acknowledge
the support of the Canada Council for the Arts for our
publishing program.

The Canada Council | Le Conseil des Arts
for the Arts | du Canada

ONTARIO ARTS COUNCIL
CONSEIL DES ARTS DE L'ONTARIO

*Title Page: A lithograph based on an 1824 painting by
Peter Rindisbacher.*

**Library and Archives Canada Cataloguing in
Publication**

Payne, Michael, 1951-
    The fur trade in Canada : an illustrated his-
tory / Michael Payne.

Includes bibliographical references and index.
ISBN 1-55028-843-1

    1. Fur trade—Canada—History. I. Title.

FC3206.P39 2004   971   C2004-903851-6

James Lorimer & Company Ltd., Publishers
35 Britain Street
Toronto, Ontario
M5A 1R7
www.lorimer.ca

Distributed in the U.S. by
Casemate
2114 Darby Road, 2nd floor
Havertown, PA
19083

Printed and bound in Canada

CONTENTS

ACKNOWLEDGEMENTS

This book is aimed at a broad readership, so references to specific authors and their works have been kept to an absolute minimum. However, anyone who writes about the fur trade has the advantage of being able to draw upon the work of literally hundreds of previous authors who have studied the subject. Fur trade history has an almost sedimentary quality, as each new book or article rests on layers of previous research effort. This book is no exception, and I would like acknowledge my enormous debt to the work other fur trade historians, anthropologists, economists, geographers and archaeologists. I would also like to acknowledge the many archives and archivists that have assisted my research on the fur trade over the past decades.

An illustrated history requires images, and a specific thanks is owed to all the archives and heritage organizations, which have given permission to use the maps, photographs and documentary art that make the text come alive. Peter Melnycky, Gerhard Ens and Bob Coutts graciously agreed to read that text and offered valuable advice on how to improve it. Any errors or omissions are, of course, the responsibility of the author alone.

I would also like to thank the staff at James Lorimer and Company for undertaking this project. A particular thanks is owed to the editors there, especially Chad Fraser, who managed to extract a manuscript while acquiring images, co-ordinating production and attending to all the other devilish details of book publication.

Finally I would like to thank family and friends. Over the years, they have put up with more pelts and hides from me than a chief factor at Red River.

INTRODUCTION

Missi picoutau amiscou (The beaver makes everything)

In 1634, the missionary Father Paul Le Jeune was living among the Montagnais, or the Innu as they are now known. The Innu were among the first Aboriginal peoples to be drawn into the fur trade, and they had considerable experience by 1634 with Europeans and their odd obsession with furs. Le Jeune quoted one of his hosts as saying in jest: "Missi picoutau amiscou." Le Jeune translated the comment as meaning something like "Le castor fait toutes choses parfai[t]ement bien, il nous fai[t] des chaudières, des haches, des é[p]ées, des couteaux, du pain, bref il fait tout" [The beaver does everything perfectly well: it makes kettles, hatchets, swords, knives, bread; and in short, it makes everything].

It is not easy to summarize over 500 years of trading activity in a single phrase, but Le Jeune's Innu host came about as close as anyone could. Of course the beaver did not make absolutely everything. Foxes, fishers, muskrats, bears, buffalo, elk, and a host of other animals with skins, furs, and meat that could be used in trade also "made" some of the goods

Aboriginal peoples acquired. Still, as this comment makes clear, the fur trade always involved Aboriginal peoples as producers and consumers. They were involved in the trade as traders in their own right, as employees of fur trade companies, and as members of fur trade families. In fact, in most regions of Canada, the first person to show up in a hunting camp looking for furs to trade would not have been a European or Canadien, but a Cree, Innu, Huron, Blackfoot, Chipewyan, or other First Nations trader. Historian Gerald Friesen has described the fur trade up to at least the early 19th century as really two parallel, but distinct, trades, "one controlled by the natives and the other shared by Indians and European entrepreneurs."

The fur trade also brought together "mix't bands of many nations," as one fur trade commentator put it. Among others, English, French, Scots, Americans, Canadiens, Métis, Iroquois, and Orcadians from the Orkney Islands all worked in the fur trade. It was very much a multilingual, multicultural enterprise, and evidence of this can be found in the specialized vocabulary and material culture of fur trade life.

Canot de Maitre, 1882 painting by J. Halkett.

Fur traders wore *capots* and *moccasins*, travelled using *carioles*, *toboggans,* and *carts*, and ate *pemmican*, *bannock*, and *tripe de roche* — although the latter, lichens, only when truly desperate.

The fur trade was marked by both competition and cooperation between French- and English-speaking traders and between companies based in Montreal and London. It was a business, but it was also a way of life, and the fur trade produced some of the oldest settled communities on the continent. The main administrative centre for the Hudson's Bay Company, York Factory, was established in the same year as Philadelphia, and Quebec City, first established as a fur trade centre, is older than all but a handful of other North American cities.

In many respects the fur trade serves as something of a metaphor for Canadian history. Some Canadian historians, such as Harold Innis, even argued that the fur trade literally "made" Canada. In 1930 Innis wrote, "Canada emerged as a political entity with boundaries largely determined by the fur trade…The significance of the fur trade consisted in its determination of the geographical framework [of Canada]."

This may overstate the case — many major fur trade centres, including Detroit, Grande Portage, and Fort Vancouver, are not in Canada now — but the fur trade was a very significant factor in ensuring the United States of America and Canada emerged as separate transcontinental nations. So the beaver may not have actually made everything, but the pursuit of its fur for trade certainly had enormous historical consequences — consequences that we still live with today.

Ojibwa hood made of stroud, a British-made cloth.

1

IN THE BEGINNING — THE FUR TRADE TO 1608

The fur trade was not a distinctly European invention. It began as a part of larger and very ancient patterns of trade among Aboriginal peoples. This partially explains why so many Aboriginal groups across North America adapted to trade with Europeans so quickly. The newly arrived European traders simply tapped into already-existing trade networks throughout the continent. They altered these trade networks and introduced new products, but they did not begin trade, nor were they always the ones actively seeking out trade opportunities.

No one can say exactly where and when the fur trade began or who was responsible for starting it. We do know that for thousands of years Aboriginal peoples traded goods among themselves and that this trade was well organized, extensive, and common. Archaeological sites and the oral traditions of different First Nations make it clear that long before any European tried to trade axes for beaver pelts, trade goods were being exchanged over routes that extended hundreds, even thousands, of kilometres. Archaeologists have found obsidian projectile points at sites scattered across the Canadian Prairies, and the volcanic glass can be traced to specific sources in Wyoming and the interior of British

Painting of an Aboriginal hunter from the Maritimes, by Henri Beau based on earlier images.

Columbia. Copper from Lake Superior and from the Coppermine River in the Northwest Territories turns up in sites hundreds of kilometres from its source. Other products, such as shells used for decoration and, in the form of wampum, for ceremonial and diplomatic purposes; flint; and other stone used for tools were also traded over long distances and in large quantities.

Because stone, shell, and metal all tend to survive better in archaeological sites than perishable items such as furs, leather, and foodstuffs, the extent of trade in these latter items cannot be traced with assurance. Nonetheless, northern boreal forest peoples undoubtedly traded furs with their more southerly neighbours in return for corn, stone for tool making, shells, and other goods. Early historical records also suggest that some individuals, and even entire bands, specialized in trade. The name *Odawa*, or *Ottawa*, was used by an Algonquin First Nation and literally means "traders." Other First Nations with strong trading traditions include the Huron/Wendat, the Mandan/Hidatsa, the Nootka, the Cree, and the Chipewyan, among others. There were even distinct trade languages, such as the Chinook "jargon" used on Canada's west coast.

This language, based on words from many languages, developed to facilitate trade between different First Nations, and a version of Chinook Jargon may well predate the arrival of Europeans.

Most of us are used to thinking about Europeans as explorers and discoverers of the New World. What is less well known is that Aboriginal groups also purposely sought out Europeans, engaging in long voyages of exploration and discovery in order to meet these new people. For example, in the mid-19th century, oral histories of how the Anishinabeg, or Ojibwa, first met Europeans were collected. These accounts date back to the establishment of the first French trading settlements on the St. Lawrence River in the early 1600s. Although they lived far in the interior, the Ojibwa heard stories that some strange new people had recently appeared. A council was held, and it was decided to send an expedition from the upper Great Lakes to the St. Lawrence to see who these people were. After weeks of travel, the expedition finally found an abandoned hut surrounded by stumps that seemed to have been cut down

The most commonly used, but purely imaginary, portrait of Jacques Cartier. By F. Riss, 1844. No authentic portraits of Cartier are known to exist.

"by the teeth of a colossal beaver." Continuing on, the explorers reached a small settlement filled with people they thought resembled squirrels, as they kept all their food and goods in wooden containers shaped like hollow trees. The two groups exchanged gifts and trade items. Their initial curiosity satisfied, the Ojibwa explorers returned home. Like the early European explorers who brought strange and exotic items back as both souvenirs and proof of their discoveries, the Ojibwa returned with a collection of strange and fascinating goods, such as cloth and metal knives and axes. On their return, more councils were held as the Ojibwa tried to work out what these new products were good for and what benefit there might be in future dealings with these new people. In short, the Ojibwa behaved in almost exactly the same way as people in France

and England did to the return of Cartier and Cabot.

In addition to reminding us just how hard it is for anyone meeting new peoples to make sense of the language, culture, and behaviour of those peoples — and thus just how cautious we should be in taking European explorers' accounts of early contacts with Aboriginal groups at face value — these stories make it clear that Aboriginal peoples were just as much explorers and discoverers as Europeans in the early contact period. Far from the "old" world of Europe discovering the "new" world of North America, historian Sarah Carter argues that "the history of culture contact in North America is the story of how two old worlds, each containing many diverse peoples, met, in many cases collided, and from that time on were intertwined."

In 1534 Jacques Cartier described a trade encounter near Chaleur Bay. His ships met a large party of Indians, probably Mi'kmaq, who immediately held up furs on sticks to attract Cartier and his men. Despite some initial fear on the part of the French that led them to fire two small cannons and two "fire-lances" above the advancing Indians, the next day trade commenced. Cartier described the response of the Mi'kmaq to securing "iron wares and other commodities" as highly enthusiastic:

> They bartered all they had to such an extent that all went back naked without anything on them; and they made signs to us that they would return on the morrow with more furs.

This story makes it clear that it was Cartier and his crew who were initially reluctant to trade, not the Mi'kmaq.

The Mi'kmaq obviously knew that Europeans on ships had useful items to trade and that they would exchange those goods for furs. The reason why the Mi'kmaq and other First Nations in the Gulf of St. Lawrence and Atlantic coast areas knew this is because, by 1534, they had already had considerable contact with European fishermen, particularly from northern France and England. The early European fur trade was really an offshoot of the cod fishery.

Basque, Portuguese, and Spanish fishermen from southern Europe had access to large supplies of salt produced by evaporating seawater. This meant they could preserve their catches offshore. English and northern French fishermen had to purchase salt, so they developed a shore-based fishery that used a combination of drying and smaller quantities of salt to preserve catches. Because English and French fishermen built coastal fishing stations in Atlantic Canada, they inevitably came into contact with Aboriginal peoples who also travelled to the coast to fish in summer. As in Cartier's experience, these casual contacts often led to trade. They also helped make London, Paris, and several merchant towns in northern France early European centres for the North American fur trade and manufacturing that used furs.

According to Harold Innis, initially the trade "was of minor importance and incidental to fishing." In part this was because there was limited demand for furs in Europe until the later 16th century. At first, the largest European market was for the so-called "fancy" furs, such as marten, mink, and ermine, which were prized for their appearance and used for luxury clothing. Beaver would later dominate the fur trade because of a particular quality of its fur. If you look at the inner hairs of a beaver pelt through a microscope, you will see a rough, almost barbed surface. This means the fur can be made to make a particularly fine quality felt. European hat makers knew about beaver felt, since beaver had long been

The trading encounter at the Bay of Chaleur between Cartier and a large party of native peoples on 3 July, 1534. Painted by Theodore Gudin, based on Cartier's description of the event.

trapped in Russia and Scandinavia. However, by the 1500s, beavers were effectively extinct in western Europe, and North American supplies were a valuable alternative. It took some years for beaver-felt hats to become popular, but by the 1580s, European merchants were outfitting expeditions specifically to trade for beaver and other furs.

Aboriginal groups killed beaver for food and to make clothing. For reasons of warmth, beaver robes were worn with the fur side in. Over time, the long outer guard hairs of the pelt wore away from constant contact with human skin. The fur that remained was a soft, downy inner hair, and the exterior skin became pliable and well greased from use. French traders called beaver pelts that had been used as robes *castor gras,* or "greasy beaver," and distinguished these pelts from ordinary beaver pelts, which were called *castor sec,* or dry beaver. Hatters discovered that these well-worn robes were ideal for hat making. Because they were worth more to hatters, castor gras was also worth more to traders.

Aboriginal groups on the Atlantic coast also adopted different approaches to the possibility of trade with European fishermen. Some, such as the Mi'kmaq and Innu, embraced the opportunity to trade with Europeans and apparently sought out trade opportunities. Members of these First Nations began to trade goods they had acquired from Europeans to people living further inland for more furs, establishing themselves as "middleman" traders in their own right. Other groups, such as the Beothuk in Newfoundland, appear to have avoided trade contact. Because coastal fishermen returned to Europe in the autumn, at first the Beothuk were able to collect metal and other materials from abandoned fishing stations. They fashioned this scavenged material into their own tools and other products without having to collect furs for trade.

This strategy worked well so long as fishermen returned to

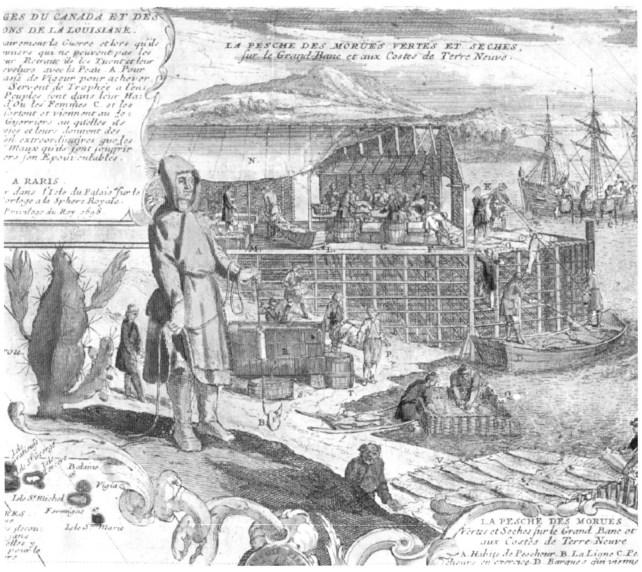

Inset of "A View of a Stage and also of Manner of Fishing for, Curing and Drying Cod at Newfoundland" on "A Map of North America," Herman Moll.

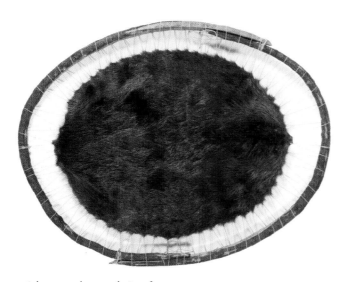

A beaver pelt on a drying frame.

Europe every year. When fishing stations were occupied year-round, the Beothuk came into increasing conflict with Europeans. Kept away from the coast by fishermen and facing competition from European and other Aboriginal trappers in the interior of Newfoundland, the numbers of Beothuk began to decline. There are several accounts of violent confrontations between groups of Beothuk and Europeans, and the Beothuk may have been subject to newly introduced diseases as well. In 1823, three starving Beothuk women surrendered to a settler and were taken to St. John's. They may well have been the last of their people, because no other Beothuk were ever encountered. Two of the women died soon after surrendering. The third, Shanawdithit, lived long enough to give an account of her vanished people's way of life before she too died in 1829.

As demand for fur grew in Europe, traders could no longer rely on casual contacts with Aboriginal groups to supply the necessary volume of furs. Instead, European merchants worked with Aboriginal middleman traders to establish regular times and locations for trade. The French, in particular, established a number of early trading centres on the Atlantic coast and in the Gulf of St. Lawrence. For example, archaeological investigations at Ile aux Basques, a French Basque fishing site occupied from 1584 to about 1637, indicate that this site was also used for trade with Aboriginal

Beaver hunting in Canada, 1777-78, Chiedel.

groups. Tadoussac was even more important. Located at the mouth of the Saguenay River, it was a natural trade centre and was apparently used for that purpose long before Europeans took an interest in furs. Aboriginal traders, most of them Innu, or "Montagnais" as the French called them, used the river to bring furs from what is now northern Quebec and Labrador to meet French merchants at Tadoussac. By the late 1500s this was an annual occurrence, and in 1600 Pierre Chauvin tried to found what most historians consider the first true trading-post settlement in what is now Canada at Tadoussac.

In 1603, after Chauvin's venture failed, Pierre du Gua de

Monts, another French merchant, was granted a royal patent to establish a colony and develop trade on the Atlantic coast. De Monts first tried to build a trading-post settlement in 1604 at Ile Ste. Croix on what is now the border between Maine and New Brunswick. The settlement barely survived the winter, and in 1605 de Monts moved his operations to Port Royale on the Annapolis Basin in what is now Nova Scotia. Although briefly abandoned in 1607 when de Monts lost his trade monopoly in the region, Port Royale was later resettled. It proved to be a good location for both trading and settlement and served for many years as one of the centres of French Acadia.

When forced to abandon Port Royale in 1607, de Monts turned his attention to the St. Lawrence River region again. Although he himself never returned to North America, his lieutenant Samuel de Champlain took over management of de Monts's fur trade interests. Champlain had long believed that the St. Lawrence River region was the real key to the trade. It was virtually impossible to enforce a trade monopoly on the Atlantic coast, with so much coastline and so many fishermen and other merchants. As a result, royal patents granting trade privileges in return for establishing colonies had little effect. A settlement on the St. Lawrence was another matter altogether. The region had potential to produce far more and better furs, while trade privileges could be enforced with slightly more ease.

Champlain established what would become the first really successful trading-post settlement and the capital of New France — Quebec — in 1608. This was a critical turning point in the history of the fur trade in Canada. The new settlement could not hope to produce fish in competition with Atlantic fisheries. Instead, Champlain's settlement would have to rely on the fur trade as its economic base.

Sieur de Monts.

Examples of a bicorne hat.

2

Fateful Decisions — The Fur Trade, 1608–1663

Champlain's settlement at Quebec would change the course of fur trade history. The real focus of the fur trade moved inland. Although furs were still traded in Atlantic Canada (and wild and ranched furs remain a small but significant part of the economies of the Maritime provinces to this day), the old ship- and fishery-based trade gave way to one based on permanent settlements located on the St. Lawrence River–Great Lakes drainage system.

The arrival of Champlain at Quebec, painted by George Agnew Reid in 1909.

Champlain's choice of Quebec as the site for his trading-post settlement was strategically brilliant. Quebec is a natural fortress and harbour, and it was ideally located to control trade. It commanded a huge hinterland, stretching inland along the lakes and rivers that flow into the St. Lawrence. Trade goods entering this region and furs leaving it had little choice but to pass by or through Quebec. The only real rival to Quebec and the St. Lawrence River as a route to the interior was a

This early iron axe and hammer was found in Ontario. It was apparently traded between Aboriginal peoples there.

southerly route using the Hudson and Mohawk rivers to reach the Great Lakes and Ottawa River. For roughly half a century, from 1608 to 1663, the story of the fur trade is the story of the struggle to control trade and transportation routes to the interior and to master the technology and logistics of this trade.

There was little in Champlain's 1608 settlement to foreshadow all this. Champlain describes it as three two-storey buildings "three fathoms long, and two and a half wide." He also built a larger storehouse with cellar. Aware of the threat from rival traders and potentially hostile Aboriginal groups, Champlain tried to make his settlement secure. He joined the buildings together and built a gallery around their outside walls. He also surrounded the post with a large moat, mounted cannons, and cleared land to plant crops. Then he and his tiny garrison of 24 men settled in for the winter.

De Monts and Champlain never really secured their trade monopoly with this post. The settlement barely

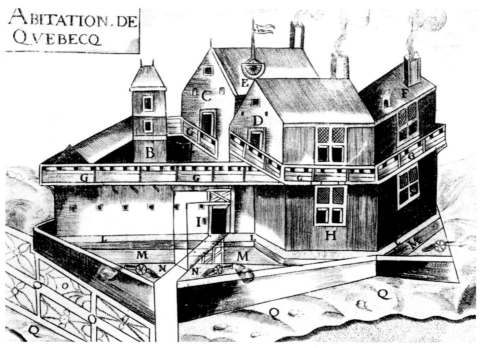

ABITATION. DE QVEBECQ

Champlain's Habitation at Quebec, 1608, drawn by Champlain himself to illustrate his published journals in 1613.

Also known as the Five Nations, or the League of Iroquois, the confederacy was later joined by a sixth nation — the Tuscaroras displaced from North Carolina in the early 1700s. The member nations of the Iroquois Confederacy originally lived in the area stretching from the Hudson River to the Finger Lakes and Lake Ontario in what is now New York State. The Mohawk lived on the eastern boundary of this area and the Seneca on the west. The Iroquois likened their league to a longhouse, so the Mohawk were known as "the keepers of the eastern door" and the Seneca as the "keepers of the western door." The Onondaga, Oneida, and Cayuga lived in between. Interestingly, the Huron/Wendat were also an Iroquoian people — culturally and linguistically very similar to the five Iroquois nations — and a confederacy of five distinct nations as well.

survived the first winter; just eight men were left alive in spring. However, by being there and available to trade, Champlain had a major advantage over his rivals. He also used his growing contacts with his fur suppliers — the Montagnais/Innu of northern Quebec, the Algonquins from the Ottawa River area, and the Huron/Wendat (or Ouendat) from further inland — to build an economic, political, and military alliance. These First Nations did trap furs, but they were also active traders. They exchanged European goods acquired in trade — among other products — with other Aboriginal groups unwilling or unable to reach Quebec or coastal fishing and trade sites.

This meant Champlain was dependent upon the goodwill of his Aboriginal trading partners, which also meant he was tied to their military and diplomatic concerns. The Hurons, Algonquins, and Montagnais were enemies of the Iroquois Confederacy, at the time an alliance of five distinct peoples: the Mohawk, the Onondaga, the Oneida, the Cayuga, and the Seneca.

In order to cement trade ties, Champlain and two companions agreed to join an attack on the Iroquois in 1609. The war party travelled along the Richelieu River to what is now Lake Champlain, where it met with an equally large party of Iroquois. There was little to separate this encounter from previous ones except that this time the Algonquins and Montagnais had three Frenchmen and their arquebuses, an early form of firearm, with them.

The Iroquois, expecting nothing unusual, were armed with bows and arrows and protected by light armour "woven from cotton thread and wood." Effective against arrows or spears, this armour offered no protection from shot. Champlain advanced to the front of his allies and fired an arquebus loaded with four musket balls. This first shot had an astounding effect. Two of the leading Iroquois chiefs immediately fell dead and a third warrior was wounded. When a second Frenchman fired from the neighbouring woods, the Iroquois were thrown into a panic. They had never encountered such weapons before, and fled.

It was a great victory for his allies, but it would turn out to be a costly one for Champlain and the French. It is said that sometimes one has to make enemies in order to make friends, but making an enemy of the Iroquois would have enormous consequences for the French fur trade. The Iroquois controlled access to the interior along the Hudson-Mohawk River route and thus offered a kind of natural rivalry to the middleman trade of the Hurons and Algonquins. More important, the close ties of the Iroquois Confederacy enabled the five allied nations to act with a coordination and purpose that few other First Nations could match.

They proved to be formidable enemies indeed, as the shock of Champlain's guns quickly wore off. In a second battle in 1610 near Sorel, Quebec, the Iroquois were expecting guns and very nearly defeated Champlain and his allies. Moreover, the Iroquois were soon able to acquire their own guns, first from Dutch then English traders. Subsequent engagements, such as the attack on an Onondagan village in 1615 that saw Champlain wounded, undermine the assumption that firearms were a decisive factor in early conflicts between European and Aboriginal peoples.

The full consequences of these events were not immediately obvious, and from 1609 to 1627 Champlain struggled to make his settlement a success. It was not an easy task. The French government granted trade monopolies and then withdrew them with dizzying speed. In most cases, special trade rights were unenforceable anyhow. With both royal government and merchant companies reluctant to invest in Quebec, the settlement staggered along. Champlain's garrison of 8 survivors in 1609 had grown to just 107 people in 1627.

Champlain and his associates did make a number of

Champlain's first encounter with the Iroquois on Lake Champlain in 1609, drawn by Champlain himself, 1613.

important strides, however. Champlain encouraged young men such as Etienne Brûlé to travel inland with Aboriginal groups to learn their languages and way of life. In this way the French learned more about the geography and resources of the interior and began a slow process of adopting — and adapting — Aboriginal technology to support the fur trade. Champlain also undertook his own voyages of "discovery," although historians are now inclined to point out that these were more like guided tours. He travelled to the Ottawa River

Ste. Marie among the Hurons national historic site, near Midland, Ontario.

in 1613, and in 1615 he reached Huronia, on the shores of Georgian Bay.

Also in 1615, he invited a group of Recollet missionaries to Quebec to establish missions among Aboriginal groups. When the first missions had little success, Jesuit priests were recruited in 1625 to pursue evangelical efforts with more vigour. Missionary activities were inextricably linked to the fur trade. They were often seen as the advance guard of the fur trade. For example, missionaries demanded that only "Christian" Indians be allowed to acquire firearms. Perhaps most important, Jesuit missionary activities at Ste. Marie among the Hurons, near modern Midland, Ontario, caused serious social and political tension between converts and other Hurons. This tension helped destabilize Huron society and later aided the Iroquois in defeating the Hurons.

The tentative beginnings of Champlain's settlement received a boost in 1627, and then a huge setback in 1629. In 1627, the government of France led by Cardinal Richelieu created a single merchant company, the Company of New France, to handle all trade by land and sea with Quebec for a period of 15 years. The company was also given ownership of all the land in the St. Lawrence Valley — one of the first instances of a common, if remarkably cavalier, disdain for Aboriginal land rights on the part of European monarchs. In return, the company was supposed to settle at least 200 new colonists a year.

Unfortunately for the Company of New France, its ambitious plans ran afoul of rising tensions between England and France. In 1628, open hostilities broke out and English privateers captured several fishing vessels and supply ships bound for Quebec. In 1629, an English fleet of privateers led by the sons of English merchant Jarvis Kirke went a stage further and forced the surrender of Quebec. Champlain and his supporters were offered free passage back to France, and from 1629 to 1632 the Kirke family ran the fur trade from Quebec.

The course of Canadian history would have been quite different had the Kirkes kept Quebec, but the Treaty of St. Germain en Laye ended this colonial conflict with a property exchange. Quebec was returned to France, and ultimately to the Company of New France. In turn, this merchant company would manage the French fur trade and run the colony until 1645, when the trade monopoly was transferred yet again to a group of Canadian merchants — the Communauté des Habitants.

Champlain returned one last time to his trading-post settlement in 1633, but his time at the centre of the French fur trade was largely past. Two years later, on Christmas Day, 1635, he died at Quebec after suffering a stroke. He lived just long enough to see Quebec and the St. Lawrence fur trade returned to France, but not long enough to see his system of trade based on alliances with the Montagnais, Algonquins, and Hurons come within a hair's breadth of failing completely.

The early fur trade was based on the vastly different values different people place on products. Europeans valued furs very highly and saw the trade goods they offered in exchange as less desirable. Aboriginal groups generally reversed this economic equation. As a result, there were excellent markups to be had by Aboriginal traders exchanging European goods inland for furs. These furs then went at another steep premium when re-traded to Europeans.

That said, the fur trade was a very chancy business in the first half of the 17th century for Aboriginal and European traders alike. It was a classic "high risk, high reward" enterprise, and the risks were not limited to money. French merchants risked losing their ships and cargoes to English or Dutch interests, and vice versa. Merchants also risked losing their ships — and thus profits — at sea, and traders could risk their lives. Champlain was wounded fighting the Iroquois, and for reasons that have never been fully explained, the Hurons killed Etienne Brûlé in 1633.

Trade was even more risky for

Costumed guide at Sainte Marie among the Hurons National Historic Site.

Aboriginal middlemen. They faced all the same risks as European merchants to their cargoes of trade goods and furs. They also faced being killed by aggrieved customers and rival traders from other First Nations.

Despite these risks, between the 1620s and 1640s the Hurons emerged as the greatest source of furs for the French, while the Iroquois dominated trade with the Dutch and English. Both Hurons and Iroquois produced furs from their own territories, but they also traded for furs with other First Nations. The Hurons, in particular, were well situated to take on the role of trading with their neighbours for fur and other goods, which were then resold to the French at a profit. Historical and archaeological evidence indicates that the Hurons were adept traders long before the French arrived. Huron trade connections extended throughout much of the Great Lakes and Canadian Shield regions. The French arrival simply opened new possibilities for trade based on the Hurons' strategic location near Georgian Bay. The Hurons controlled key trade routes and thus access to French trading settlements for many of the northern First Nations of the Canadian Shield region.

The result was a curious two-part trading system. One fur trade operated almost exclusively among Aboriginal producers and purchasers. The second linked some Aboriginal producers and traders with Europeans. French, Dutch, and later English traders waited in post settlements for Aboriginal peoples to arrive with furs and other commodities to trade, while a second parallel — and in the early years much larger — system of trade took place far from any European trading enclave. Historian Gerald Friesen's idea of two distinct fur trades clearly characterizes the early trade contacts of the 1600s.

The Iroquois may have been less motivated by trade with

Twentieth-century illustration of Champlain leaving Quebec, a prisoner on Kirke's ship, by C. W. Jeffreys.

Europeans than the Hurons were, but they too saw some advantage in it. By 1663, the Iroquois traded nearly 30,000 pelts a year to the Dutch — often for guns. As a result, by the late 1640s, the Iroquois were much better armed than the Hurons. Where the Iroquois possessed roughly 500 trade guns, the Hurons had no more than about one-quarter of that number. The balance of military power shifted dramatically, and in the 1640s, the Iroquois launched a series of attacks on the allies of the French, especially the Hurons.

Initially these attacks were limited to ambushing the flotillas of Huron and Algonquin canoes bringing furs along the Ottawa River to Quebec and a new settlement at Montreal, established in 1642.

By the late 1640s, the Iroquois campaign was aimed directly at the main villages of Huronia. The Hurons were weakened after several major epidemics and were in social turmoil because of the activities of missionaries. With depleted numbers and unable to coordinate a response between Christians and non-Christians, the Huron Confederacy collapsed in 1649, and with it France's main source of furs from the interior.

Although many Hurons were killed or captured by the Iroquois, they did not disappear as a people. Many, especially those who had become Christians, took up land around the French settlements in the St. Lawrence Valley. Others fled west and south. The fleeing Hurons were incorporated into other bands or formed new ones such as the Wyandot, another variation of the name *Wendat*, of the Ohio River.

With the Hurons gone as a significant rival, the Iroquois turned their attention to the French and their remaining trade partners. Far from being intimidated by the French, the Iroquois attacked and harried French settlers throughout the St. Lawrence Valley. They also defeated in quick succession most of the main non-Iroquois peoples in the Lower Great Lakes-St. Lawrence River system.

The question of what motivated the Iroquois to attack the Hurons and the French with such persistence and ferocity

Mohawk-Iroquois knife and sheath.

remains a lively debate among historians. For many years, most accepted what is essentially an economic and military explanation of Iroquois behaviour. The Iroquois were eager to trade with the Dutch, and after 1664 the English, on the Hudson River, especially for muskets to counteract the military advantage gained by their enemies through trade with the French.

Unfortunately for the Iroquois, their traditional lands in what is now New York State produced limited quantities of beaver and furs. According to this view, the Iroquois acted in a perfectly rational manner, using warfare to secure new supplies of furs. They did this by acquiring new territory, taking over middleman trade networks, and capturing beaver and other furs from enemy groups.

More recently, historians have advanced alternative explanations of this warfare. Many of these theories try to balance "economic" and "cultural" motives to understand Iroquois actions. Some have emphasized Iroquois political cohesion, which allowed the Iroquois first to focus their attacks on the Hurons and later the French themselves. By contrast, the Hurons were unable to mount an effective defence because disease and missionary activity had destabilized their confederacy.

Others note that the Iroquois did not really establish themselves as middleman traders, and the volume of Iroquois trade did not vastly increase during the period of these wars. Instead, the Iroquois seemed more interested in capturing prisoners than acquiring furs or territory. Perhaps the real motivation of the Iroquois was to replace their population, which was declining because of warfare and disease. Georges Sioui, a historian with a Huron/Wendat background, has argued that the Iroquois were engaged in a much larger socio-cultural struggle with the Hurons. The Iroquois represented the approach of opposition to European incursions, whereas the Hurons represented an approach of accommodation and exchange.

The Iroquois campaign dried up supplies of fur in New France and forced French fur traders into desperate new measures. Before 1649, French traders had left the collecting and transporting of furs from inland to their Aboriginal trade partners. After 1649, the French had to take on the dangerous task of trading directly with people who formerly supplied furs to the Hurons, Algonquins, and even Montagnais.

In order to do this, a new profession was created, the *coureur de bois*. In what was essentially an expansion of Champlain's old policy of sending young men such as Etienne Brûlé out to live among the Indians, the *coureurs de bois* travelled inland with supplies of trade goods to winter among First Nations bands. Over the winter they traded these goods for furs and then transported the furs down to Montreal, Quebec, Trois-Rivières, or Tadoussac. This meant running the gauntlet of Iroquois raiders, especially along the Ottawa River, with furs and life potentially at forfeit.

Louis XIV, by Hyacinthe Rigaud, 1694.

In order to be successful, the coureurs de bois had to be daring and resourceful. They also had to master Aboriginal languages and trade rituals. They needed to travel using Aboriginal technology, such as canoes, toboggans, and snowshoes. They had to dress, eat, and live like their partners and customers. Many married Aboriginal women according to the customs of First Nations, a practice later termed *mariage à la façon du pays,* or "country marriage." Champlain once told a group of his trading partners, "Our sons shall marry your daughters and together we shall form one people." His comment was remarkably prescient. These fur trade marriages would eventually become the basis for a distinctive hybrid fur trade society rooted in both Aboriginal and European cultural traditions.

The *coureurs de bois* saved the French fur trade after the destruction of Huronia and initiated a period of rapid expansion and development of the trade. Still, the colony of New France did not flourish, particularly as it was estimated that nearly 10 per cent of its population chose to live inland and work in the fur trade. By 1663, Champlain's colony had a population of just 3,000 people, compared with 70,000

American colonists.

The fur trade helped shape both the greatest strengths and weaknesses of New France. Aside from the Iroquois, the French generally developed close trade and diplomatic connections with First Nations. The economic hinterland of New France was always vast as a result, but the population lagged far behind the British colonies to the south. In an attempt to improve New France's defences and develop its potential beyond the fur trade, Louis XIV of France made it a royal colony in 1663. In practical terms, France was so far away that local administrators still largely governed the colony, but New France's becoming a royal colony would have a major impact on the fur trade.

A Recollet missionary.

3

THE STRUGGLE FOR THE NORTHERN FUR TRADE, 1663–1713

The early 1660s were a period of major changes in the fur trade. In 1664 the English captured the Dutch settlements on the Hudson River and thereafter served as the main suppliers and allies of the Iroquois. After conquering Huronia and dispersing the Hurons and most of the Hurons' allies, the Iroquois turned their attention to the main French settlements on the St. Lawrence. Whether their motive was simply to seize control over the fur trade or — more ambitiously — to push the French colonists completely out of the St. Lawrence region remains the subject of historical debate. What is not debated is that by the early 1660s New France was in danger of collapse as a result of Iroquois attacks on French fur traders and settlements.

A 17th-century illustration of Algonquins.

Quebec to help defend the colony against the Iroquois. They quickly set to work building forts along the Richelieu River and strengthening the defences of the main settlements in the colony.

Then, in a daring, if foolhardy, campaign, a force of roughly half the regiment supported by a few Canadian volunteers invaded Mohawk territory in February 1666. The invasion was not a success. The Iroquois ambushed the troops and no real damage was done except to the 60-odd men who died during the long retreat back to New France. A second invasion of Mohawk lands in September had little more success. A few abandoned villages and crops were burned, but for the most part the Iroquois simply avoided direct contact with these troops.

Becoming a royal colony signalled a shift in the degree of support and interest Champlain's old colony could expect from France, and in 1665 the first really tangible evidence of this change became apparent. In June of that year, some 1,100 members of the Carignan-Salières Regiment arrived in

In the past, some Canadian historians suggested that the arrival of these European-trained regular army forces tilted the balance of power in the Iroquois Wars and ensured the survival of New France. More recently, other historians have been skeptical of this claim. The Iroquois do not appear to have been particularly intimidated by French soldiers and

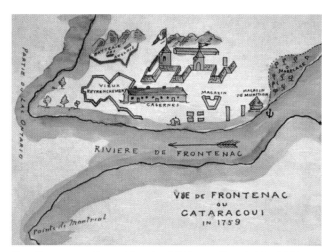

Fort Frontenac, pictured here in 1759, was founded in 1673 on Lake Ontario to serve as an inland base for the fur trade.

were quite capable of fighting them in raid and ambush warfare. Fortunately for New France, and probably the men of the regiment as well, the main military attention of the Iroquois was focused elsewhere at this time — on struggles with Algonquian groups such as the Ottawa and Ojibwa, and on warfare in the area south of Lake Erie. In 1667 the Iroquois agreed to a temporary peace with the French.

The treaty of 1667 did not end the Iroquois Wars, which flared up again in the 1680s and 1690s and threatened the settlements of New France. Warfare was not formally ended until 1701, when the Iroquois agreed to stay neutral in any future wars between the British and the French. Still, the temporary respite from attack in the late 1660s and 1670s enabled fur traders from New France to vastly increase their trading activities and expand the area of their economic influence.

The expansion of French fur trade efforts took place in the regions north and west of the Great Lakes, and south of the Great Lakes along the Mississippi River and its tributaries. In 1673 the Comte de Frontenac, governor of New France, established a fort and trading post called Fort Frontenac, or Cataraqui, at the site of what is now Kingston, Ontario. This post was to act as an inland base for the fur trade, and it was hoped that it would attract trade from the temporarily peaceful Iroquois.

That same year Father Marquette and Louis Jolliet travelled from Lake Michigan to the Mississippi River, and then along the Mississippi south to the Arkansas River before returning by way of the Illinois River to Lake Michigan. Jolliet was disappointed in his hopes of gaining the right to trade in the Illinois area, but over time French traders developed a series of posts and trading settlements in the area south and west of Detroit and along the Mississippi River. In 1679, for example, French traders built a new post at Fort Niagara. In 1682, the fur trader and explorer La Salle reached the mouth of the Mississippi River and claimed the entire region from the Great Lakes to the Gulf of Mexico for France.

The fur trade south of the Great Lakes was a very important part of the trade of New France, and it remained so until the Conquest of Quebec in 1759. Indeed, Canadian fur traders remained active in this vast area of what is now the United States until well after the American Revolution. Nonetheless, it was the fur traders operating in the area north of the Great Lakes who had the most profound impact on Canadian history.

In 1610 Henry Hudson sailed into Hudson Bay before spending a bleak winter trapped in James Bay near the Rupert River. During the winter, Hudson and his men had a couple of brief encounters with Aboriginal peoples that led to the trade of a few furs. The following year, Hudson and a few supporters were cast adrift by his mutinous crew and never

A representative collection of furs.

heard from again. The crew, however, did manage to return to England and over the next few years several new expeditions were sent to explore Hudson Bay as part of the British search for the North West Passage.

As a result of these early voyages, Hudson Bay and James Bay were known to Europeans, and it was dimly recognized that the lands surrounding these bays had potential as sources of furs. For the most part, however, European interest in

Strand of trade beads.

Hudson Bay remained focused on finding a northern sea route to Asia.

It was two French fur traders, Pierre-Esprit Radisson and Médard Chouart des Groseilliers, who realized the great trade potential of Hudson Bay. In the 1650s and early 1660s, Radisson and des Groseilliers were among the hundreds of young men from New France who travelled inland to trade for furs, often replacing Aboriginal middleman traders.

It was a risky, but potentially very profitable, business, and the authorities in New France struggled to control it by issuing a limited number of trading licences for particular areas. Radisson and des Groseilliers were unlicensed; however, this did not prevent them from trading. It merely added the risk of having their furs seized to the already lengthy list of risks they faced. Moreover, not all illegal traders had their furs taken, and the laws on illegal trade were usually enforced with a certain capricious disregard for the letter of the law.

While trading in the area north of Lake Superior, Radisson and des Groseilliers learned from their trading partners that many of the furs they were acquiring actually came from far to the north, from lands near a "Bay of the North Sea." Radisson later claimed to have travelled by canoe to this bay, but most historians now believe that this was just another example of his capacity for self-promotion.

Whether Radisson and des Groseilliers actually visited Hudson Bay or James Bay at this time probably matters very little. What does matter is that they returned to Trois-Rivières in 1660 with a huge cargo of furs and a plan to use ships to sail to Hudson Bay to trade directly with the Aboriginal peoples who lived far to the north of the Great Lakes. They fully expected to be treated as returning heroes, but instead the authorities confiscated their fortune in furs.

It is not entirely surprising that Radisson and des Groseilliers were unable initially to interest merchants in New France to back their idea. Direct trade through Hudson Bay

Left: A replica of the Nonsuch, *an exhibit at Winnipeg's Manitoba Museum.*

would strike at the economic foundations of New France. There would be no need to transship furs and trade goods through the St. Lawrence, and thus less need for the colony and less business for its merchants. By 1662, Radisson and des Groseilliers had decided to try their luck elsewhere.

They first tried to interest merchants in Boston in a direct trading voyage to Hudson Bay before shifting their efforts to London in 1665. As experienced fur traders, Radisson and des Groseilliers cut rather romantic figures in Restoration London, and they had some success in attracting support from court and merchant backers. In 1668, a trade expedition to Hudson Bay was organized, with Radisson and des Groseilliers as key figures. Two small ships, the *Eaglet* and the *Nonsuch,* were outfitted with trade goods and set sail for Hudson Bay. The plan was to winter at the "Bottom of the Bay," on what is now James Bay, and trade furs over the winter before returning to London the following year.

The *Eaglet,* with Radisson aboard, was forced back by bad weather, but the *Nonsuch,* commanded by Zachariah Gillam and with des Groseilliers aboard, reached Hudson Bay. The expedition sailed to the Bottom of the Bay and settled in for the winter at the mouth of the Rupert River. Gillam, des Groseilliers, and the *Nonsuch*'s crew managed not only to survive the winter but to acquire enough furs to prove that

Hudson's Bay Company account books from the 1700s.

An early Hudson's Bay Company post, by L.P. Hurd.

Radisson and des Groseilliers's idea of direct trade through Hudson Bay had real potential. After returning to London, des Groseilliers was able to secure enough support to justify creating a new fur trade company.

On May 2, 1670, King Charles II signed a royal charter creating the new company. This was, of course, the storied "Governor and Company of Adventurers of England Tradeing into Hudsons Bay," or the Hudson's Bay Company. In addition to creating the company and installing Charles's "Deare and entirely Beloved Cousin" Prince Rupert as governor, the charter also granted the new enterprise some significant benefits. In return for a purely nominal payment of "two Elkes and two Black beavers," to be paid to the Crown any time a reigning monarch actually visited the territories so airily granted, the company was given exclusive trade and other rights throughout the entire drainage basin of Hudson Bay — in perpetuity.

Depot building, York Factory, photographed in 1990.

As has often been pointed out, this region represents about one-third the total area of modern Canada.

Of course, it cost Charles nothing to make a generous grant in an area that England neither owned nor controlled, and if the charter for the new company attracted investors, so much the better. Initially, the Hudson's Bay Company's charter rights meant very little. French traders never accepted the validity of the charter, nor did other later English and Canadian trading companies. Certainly the people who lived in the areas Charles had given away would have registered some dismay at its provisions, had they known what the charter said. However, when the HBC finally surrendered its trade and land rights in 1869 through 1870 as part of the transfer of Rupert's Land to Canada, the company was richly rewarded for what King Charles granted in 1670.

The new company quickly established a number of forts at the mouths of rivers flowing into Hudson Bay and James Bay: Rupert House, Moose Fort, Albany House, Severn House, and Port Nelson, which would later become York Factory. Radisson and des Groseilliers, however, profited less from their plans than the English

Reproduction of a Montagnais-style toboggan.

aristocrats and merchants who invested in the new company. Within a few years both des Groseilliers and Radisson were back working for French fur trade companies, and 1682 they helped found the Compagnie du Nord, a French equivalent of the the Hudson's Bay Company. By 1684 des Groseilliers was retired, and in 1685 Radisson was back working for the HBC.

In his memoirs, composed after his retirement in 1687, Radisson described himself and his fellow fur traders as living like "Caesars of the Wilderness," but the reality of the life in the early fur trade was less romantic. For one thing, company fortunes could change with dizzying speed. The HBC declared its first dividend of 50 percent for its shareholders in 1684, and two years later it lost most of its posts. In 1686, Pierre de Troyes led an audacious overland expedition against the English posts on James Bay. After travelling up the Ottawa River and then by lake and river over the height of land to the Abitibi River, de Troyes and his party of about 90 troops and supporting voyageurs descended on a completely unprepared Moose Fort. After capturing Moose, the French also captured Rupert House and Albany House and kept these posts until 1693. The Compagnie du Nord built a post, Fort Bourbon, on the

Shooting the Rapids, by Frances Hopkins, 1879. This painting suggests the skill and daring of fur trade canoemen. Montreal-based traders had to master such skills in order to trade in the interior.

Hayes River in 1682, only to see it handed over to the HBC with Radisson's connivance in 1685. Between the 1680s and 1713, most posts on Hudson Bay and James Bay changed hands at least once as the fortunes of colonial war and treaty negotiations dictated.

It was not until the Treaty of Utrecht, which ended the War of Spanish Succession in 1713, that the Hudson's Bay Company emerged as the sole fur trade company operating on Hudson and James bays. Historians generally treat the Treaty of Utrecht as the high-water mark of French colonial expansion in North America. After 1713, French fur trade interests abandoned the idea of a northern ship-based trade to concentrate on their growing control of the Great Lakes-St. Lawrence system.

For the next half-century, the basic structure of the fur trade in the interior of North America was set. English traders operated at the margins of the French trade from posts on the Hudson-Mohawk River system to the south and from posts in the north located at the mouths of rivers flowing into Hudson and James bays. French fur trade interests dominated

a huge region stretching north from the St. Lawrence River into what is now northern Quebec and Labrador, then west into much of what is now northern Ontario, and south of the Great Lakes into the Illinois and Mississippi River basins.

Just as importantly, basic approaches to trade were also set during the period from roughly 1663 to 1713. English trading companies on both Hudson Bay and the Hudson River took advantage of their access to good-quality trade goods at low prices. English traders could offer good prices for furs compared with most French traders. This helped the Hudson's Bay Company develop a post-based style of trade. Posts were established on Hudson Bay and James Bay at the mouths of major rivers, and it was expected that Aboriginal groups would bring their furs to these posts to trade. It was not the most ambitious or aggressive of approaches, but it did keep the costs of production down. In the case of the HBC, much of the cost — including time and labour — of transporting furs and trade goods was really borne by Aboriginal producers and middleman traders. It also meant that English traders were able to establish themselves in small trading-post settlements that limited contact with Aboriginal groups — at least at first.

By contrast, French traders had to adopt a different approach to overcome their disadvantage in prices they could offer on furs and key trade goods. Interior forts served as bases for traders who often travelled out to live among Aboriginal groups and collect furs at their source. This style of trade, known as trading *en derouine,* involved individual traders trading on their own account or on behalf of other merchants who advanced trade goods in return for a share of any furs received. Trading *en derouine* meant living much of the year in the camps of different Aboriginal bands, and it was the French traders who absorbed most of the costs of transporting trade goods inland to their customers and furs out to European markets. Not surprisingly, French fur traders established close ties with their trade partners, and they pushed the trade inland in search of new markets. They usually mastered Aboriginal languages, acquired a range of "country" skills from canoeing to hunting, and many had families in the interior.

The Hudson's Bay Company experimented with letting its employees take wives to the first bayside posts, but it very quickly gave this up as a bad idea. Instead, the company adopted a policy that historians Jennifer Brown and Sylvia Van Kirk have characterized as a kind of "military monasticism." The company organized its posts on a model of military ranks, dividing employees into "officers" and "men" and establishing complex hierarchies of pay, food, clothing, and accommodation. Everything — from what and where the employees ate to the kind of work they did — was dependent upon their position in the post hierarchy.

The "monasticism" part of the policy meant company employees were also theoretically prohibited from forming relationships with women from neighbouring Aboriginal bands. This prohibition was not enforced with any consistency. Some post governors tolerated, perhaps even encouraged, such family ties. Others claimed the privilege of

Portrait of Sa Ga Yeath Qua Pieth Tow by John Verelst, painted in 1710.

enjoying "marriage" with a woman, or even more than one woman, but only for themselves. Others struggled to control and suppress any sign of "immorality" at their posts. Whatever their feelings, however, families and children in the original the Hudson's Bay Company tradition could not be acknowledged until the late 18th century. As a result, post records actually hide the existence of families, and wives and children had little choice but to return to their Aboriginal families when husbands and fathers died or returned to Britain.

By contrast, French traders very early on recognized that strong kinship ties through marriage and family could have great advantages. Inland traders rarely married according to the tenets of the Roman Catholic Church, but they did form both casual and long-term attachments to Aboriginal women according to the customs and values of those women's societies. Women brought a range of vital skills to these relationships. They made clothing, prepared furs, collected food, and helped traders master new languages. Without them, French traders could not have survived inland so far from the settlements of the St. Lawrence River. No less importantly, traders working *en derouine* were often trading with people to whom they were related — a significant advantage over the English, who might offer better prices but no personal connection. By the early 1700s, there is evidence of an emerging population of mixed European and Aboriginal ancestry closely tied to both the fur trade and New France in the Great Lakes area.

It is clear that by the early 1700s there was not one but many fur trades — the fur trade of Hudson Bay, the fur trade of the St. Lawrence and Great Lakes, and an ongoing fur trade among Aboriginal peoples. Some of the early middleman traders, such as the Hurons, were largely replaced, but in their stead new Aboriginal groups were pushing their fur trade north and west beyond the Great Lakes and Hudson Bay, and south into the lands of the Mississippi, Ohio, and Illinois River systems.

4

THE FUR TRADE REACHES THE SASKATCHEWAN RIVER, 1713–1763

In 1713, the prospects for French fur traders did not look particularly promising. They had given their posts on Hudson Bay back to their English competitors, and French merchants faced a glut of furs on the market. The precarious state of the fur trade in 1713 reflects the complexity in relations between Aboriginal groups and European traders in the early 18th century.

During the colonial wars of the previous decades, France used the fur trade to support military and diplomatic objectives. Trade secured alliances with powerful Aboriginal groups and thus helped protect the colony of New France. It meant that the fur trade could never be treated as a purely business proposition. New France depended upon its Aboriginal allies, and this relationship gave those allies considerable power when it came to trade.

In fact, the question of who was dependent upon whom in the early fur trade has no simple answer. For years historians and anthropologists confidently assumed that the fur trade encouraged rapid technological and cultural change among Aboriginal peoples. According to this view, metal pots, knives, axes, and guns were superior to any equivalents made from stone, wood, bone, or sinew, and thus highly desirable. People who

An English trade rifle.

had access to guns or metal knives would quickly lose the ability to hunt using bows and arrows or to fashion knives from flint or obsidian. Aboriginal peoples would become dependent upon a regular supply of trade goods, perhaps within a generation. It was believed that this process was virtually inevitable, and that Aboriginal society after Aboriginal society followed the same path into technological dependency and cultural decline.

But did the situation in 1713 actually support such a view? It is possible to argue that fur traders were just as dependent, or even more so, on their trading partners? Living in new and sometimes hostile environments, European traders had to rely to Aboriginal peoples to supply much of their food, clothing and shelter. Fur traders leaned heavily on Aboriginal technologies. Canoes, toboggans, snowshoes, and moccasins were just a few of the dozens of material goods fur traders had to acquire from their trading partners or learn how to make for themselves. In order to survive at a post on Hudson Bay or Lake Superior, traders had to know what foods could be eaten safely and how to preserve food supplies. Since furs had to be caught, prepared, and brought to posts by

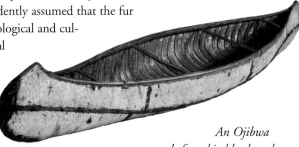

An Ojibwa canoe, made from birchbark and black spruce (or cedar).

Aboriginal groups, it is clear that dependency, if it existed at all, was a double-edged sword.

As a result, it is likely that earlier historians and anthropologists seriously overemphasized this aspect of the fur trade. The reason why there appeared to be a glut of furs on the market in 1713 was that French fur traders felt compelled to purchase virtually all the furs that were offered in trade, whether there was any market for them or not. To refuse to buy furs or to cut back on trade could threaten the military and diplomatic alliances with powerful Aboriginal groups upon which New France's existence depended. Disappointed Aboriginal traders might well decide not to come in to trade

at all or to take their furs to posts controlled by English traders. Similarly, the Hudson's Bay Company traders had to take what they were offered or risk losing their customers. In the early 18th century, it was fur producers, not buyers, who held considerable power.

Fortunately for the trading companies, the apparent glut of furs in 1713 was just that. Many had been stored for so long in warehouses that on inspection they turned out to be so damaged as to be valueless. Nevertheless, the period 1713–63 is marked by a concerted effort by both French and English fur traders to reorganize their trades to make them efficient, profitable, and slightly more market-driven. This was also a period of rapid expansion in the reach of the fur trade, in large part through the activities of Aboriginal middleman traders. By 1763 the fur trade was virtually a continent-wide enterprise involving First Nations living as far inland as the foothills of the Rockies.

After the Treaty of Utrecht, French fur traders had to give up on their plans to challenge the HBC directly with posts on Hudson Bay, but they could intercept many of the furs that otherwise would reach their English rivals. Because the Hudson's Bay Company established its posts at the mouths of the major rivers flowing into Hudson and James bays, posts built a few days' travel upriver could cut off much of the trade before Aboriginal traders reached the bayside posts. Throughout most of this period, Montreal-based fur traders kept the HBC on the defensive.

These Montreal traders, or "pedlars" as the Hudson's Bay Company employees termed them, expanded their area of trading influence south and west of the Great Lakes into the Mississippi River basin. They mixed astute diplomacy that secured the friendship and

Fort Niagara in 1891 by William Armstrong.

Fort Niagara in 2001.

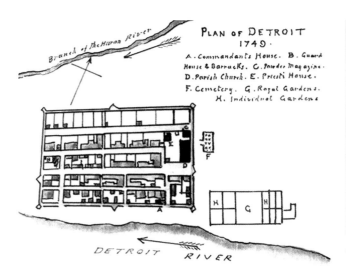

Plan of Detroit from 1749.

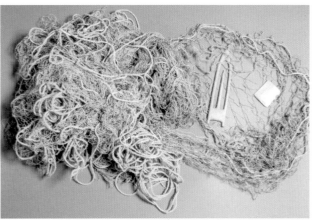

Fish formed a large part of the diet at most fur trade posts in the Canadian Shield country. Company employees used nets like this to help provide the thousands of fish a large post might consume every year.

support of Aboriginal groups in the interior with strategically located military posts. In addition to previously existing forts at places such as Detroit, the French built a fort at Niagara in 1726 and Fort Vincennes in what is now Indiana in 1727. This chain of interior forts was gradually expanded, culminating in the construction of forts near Toronto and Sault Ste. Marie in the late 1740s and early 1750s. These military forts doubled as fur trade centres that kept British settlements and traders hemmed in on the Atlantic seaboard of North America, just as posts on the rivers flowing into Hudson and James bays limited potential the HBC expansion and trade.

It was in the area north and west of Lake Superior, however, that the greatest achievements of French fur traders occurred in this period. Fur traders based in Montreal and their Aboriginal trading partners pioneered a system of trade and transportation that connected Montreal and France with fur producers living thousands of kilometres inland.

Cree and Assiniboine groups from the Lake Winnipeg area had contacted French traders prior to 1713, and routes inland from Lake Superior to what is now southern Manitoba were known in some detail by the late 1710s and early 1720s. After 1717, the French maintained a trading post at Kaministiquia, near what is now Thunder Bay at the west end of Lake Superior, and from this base a system of posts linking the plains and parklands regions with the Great Lakes was

Dog portage between the Kaministikwia River and Dog Lake, Ontario, by George Back, 1825.

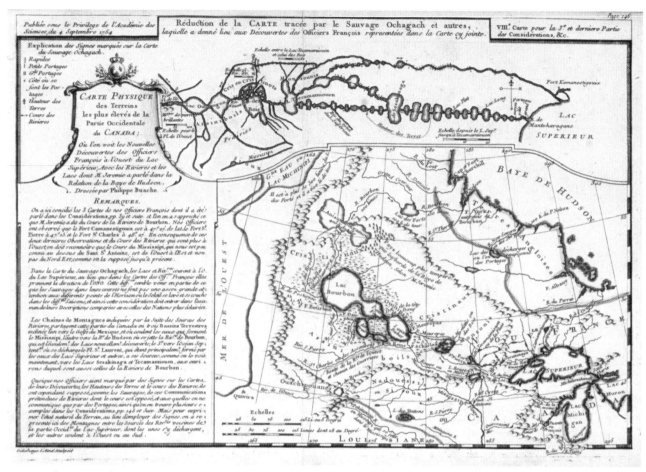

La Verendrye's map of route to Lake Winnipeg, circa 1728-29.

planned. The central figure in this story was a remarkable fur trade explorer and administrator, Pierre Gaultier de Varennes de la Vérendrye.

Based on reports from Aboriginal groups, de la Vérendrye wrote in 1729 that the area between the head of Lake Superior and the Lake of the Woods was rich in moose and marten, and that beaver was so plentiful the local Indians placed "little value on it and only collect large skins which they send to the English [on Hudson Bay]." This area could be reached by two different canoe routes that extended inland from Kaministiquia, modern Thunder Bay, and Grande Portage, which is now located in Minnesota. De la Vérendrye realized not only that this was a potentially rich area for furs

and provisions, but that building posts above Kaministiquia and Grande Portage would further undermine the Hudson's Bay Company's trade. His great stroke, however, was to tie this project to larger imperial goals, such as the search for the fabled "western sea" — a large gulf or ocean that was supposed to connect to the Pacific and the riches of the Orient. This strategy helped de la Vérendrye secure official support in Quebec and France for his plans, and it further underlines the point that prior to the late 19th century, the fur trade was not simply a commercial enterprise.

Between 1731 and 1734, de la Vérendrye and his sons constructed trading posts stretching from Lake Superior to Fort Maurepas, near the mouth of the Red River in what is now southern Manitoba. This expansion pleased the Cree and Assiniboine groups who traded at de la Vérendrye's posts, but it also provoked hostility among the Dakota (also sometimes known as Sioux), who had developed a profitable middleman trade with those same Cree and Assiniboine groups. In 1728 and again in 1730, the Dakota attacked Cree and Assiniboine groups to try to keep them from trading directly with the French at Kaministiquia. In 1736 they killed de la Vérendrye's son Jean-Baptiste and a party of voyageurs at Lake of the Woods. The result was not what the Dakota had hoped. Instead of being intimidated, de la Vérendrye began a program of aggressive expansion.

These incidents offer a reminder that the fur trade could be a dangerous business and that every time direct trade contact between European and First Nations groups was expanded north- and westwards, it usually meant some other First Nation lost its control over a middleman trade network. Once again, on the southeast edges of plains and parklands of the Canadian west, the first fur traders were not French or English, but Dakota, Ojibwa, Cree, and Assiniboine.

In 1738 de la Vérendrye travelled to the Mandans, a remarkable people who lived in villages in the Missouri River area, who grew corn, squash, and other vegetables, and who organized sophisticated trade fairs that attracted Aboriginal groups from across the northern plains. Little came of this initial contact with the Mandans, but by 1740 French fur traders were poised at the edge of two great river systems in western North America: the Saskatchewan and the Missouri. De la Vérendrye next turned his attention northwards. During the early 1740s, de la Vérendrye and his sons Pierre and Louis-Joseph established posts on Lake Winnipegosis (Lac des Prairies) and at the northern end of Lake Winnipeg. These posts, which included Forts Bourbon, Paskoyac, and Dauphin, could tap into the trade of the entire Saskatchewan River system.

In 1742, Louis-Joseph de la Vérendrye returned to the Mandan territories before travelling south and west to the edges of the Rocky Mountains. Most historians believe Louis-Joseph and his companions reached the Big Horn Mountains near what is now Yellowstone Park in Wyoming. An interesting piece of direct evidence of this journey was discovered in 1913, when a lead plaque buried by the explorers was

unearthed at Pierre, South Dakota.

This expedition indicated that there was no western sea in that direction, and the presence of a range of mountains tended to discount the idea of such a sea anywhere nearby. Still, hope remained that something might be discovered further to the north, and the de la Vérendryes calculated there were better prospects of trade in that direction as well. Pierre de la Vérendrye (père) died in 1749, but not before he began ambitious plans of exploration and trade expansion along the Saskatchewan River system.

Once again, these expeditions did not find any evidence of a western sea, although a post, Fort La Jonquière, was briefly operated in 1751-52, far to the west and within sight of the mountains. The actual location of this post is the subject of great historical debate. It has been placed at different times by different authors on both the upper South and North Saskatchewan rivers. Some have even speculated that it was located in the Calgary area.

Barring an unexpected archaeological discovery, the exact location of this westernmost expansion of the French fur trade may never be determined, but there is an interesting indication that French fur traders made direct trade contact with Blackfoot-speaking peoples in the early 1750s — if not earlier. The generic term for Europeans among Blackfoot speakers was *Napikawan,* or "Old Man person." However, they made an important distinction between French- and English-speaking Europeans. French speakers were known as "real," or "original," old man persons, suggesting that they were the first to contact Blackfoot groups.

A post located in the foothills of the Rockies proved impossible to sustain. It also showed that the mountains previously seen by Louis-Joseph de la Vérendrye apparently continued north in an unbroken chain. This put paid to any remaining belief in the possibility of discovering a western sea without having to cross the mountains, but it did not preclude trade in the area drained by the Saskatchewan River. In 1753 a post called Fort La Corne was established just east of the junction of the North and South Saskatchewan Rivers. This post was ideally suited to capture the trade of the entire region as far west as the Rockies. Fort La Corne, along with the French posts strategically located on Lakes Winnipeg and Winnipegosis, the Red and Assiniboine Rivers, and the route from the Winnipeg River to Lake of the Woods, gave de la Vérendrye's successors a clear trade advantage with the numerous and powerful First Nations of Canada's plains and parklands regions.

De la Vérendrye and his associates also worked out practical solutions to many of the economic and logistical problems presented by a long-distance fur trade. They learned that it was not possible to transport trade goods to posts on the Red River or Saskatchewan River and get furs out to Montreal in one round trip. As a result, traders from the interior posts met the men and canoes coming from Montreal at Kaministiquia and Grande Portage and exchanged cargoes for the return trip. On occasion, they may have exchanged crews as well, so that men travelling from Montreal would continue inland to winter. However, there is also evidence that some individuals began to spend year after year in the interior, travelling to Grande Portage from Fort La Corne and other inland posts with furs and then returning with supplies of trade goods.

Improvements were also made to increase the efficiency of this transport system. Canoes, especially on the Montreal–Lake Superior leg of the journey, became larger, with bigger crews and more carrying capacity. Inland depots for provisions were established and light, easily preserved but calorie-rich foods such as wild rice and corn were used to feed the canoemen. These supplies of food meant canoemen could avoid stopping to hunt or fish for provisions as they travelled.

Not that the French traders had it all their own way. In the area south and west of the Great Lakes, French fur traders faced growing competition from Anglo-American traders based in Albany, Schenectady, and other centres in the Hudson–Mohawk River and Ohio River areas. These fur trade interests played a secondary role in the fur trade at this time, but their influence would gradually increase, especially after 1763.

A fur pack ready for shipping. Companies tried to ensure packs were similar in size and weight to make transportation easier.

The Hudson's Bay Company had been seriously harmed by the loss of many of its posts for extended periods of time during the colonial wars up to 1713. Much of the company's efforts in this period had been directed at securing trade with the northern Cree, Chipewyan, and Inuit far from potential French competition in the area north and west of York Factory. The HBC was not completely content to leave all trade in the interior to the French, however.

In 1690, Henry Kelsey travelled inland with a group of Assiniboines who had visited York Factory to trade. He was charged with trying to convince the Naywatamee Poets — an unidentified people who may have been either the Hidatsa or the Gros Ventre/Atsina — to make the long journey to York Factory to trade directly with the English. Any other groups he might meet on his travels would also be offered the same encouragement. Of course, Kelsey's main mission was doomed from the start. Relations between the Naywatamee Poets and the Assiniboine were strained, even hostile, at the time. Moreover, had the Naywatamee Poets and other inland peoples even wanted to visit York Factory, the northern Cree and Assiniboine controlled the main routes to York Factory. They had little desire to let others trade directly with the English, since this would undermine their middleman trade.

Nevertheless, Kelsey was guided inland to a major Aboriginal meeting place, which he called Deering's Point. This location is usually assumed to be in the area of The Pas, and if so, it would later become a very significant fur trade centre. From Deering's Point, Kelsey travelled further inland. His journals are too cryptically written to know with assurance where he actually travelled, but he does describe animals and landscape that suggest he reached the prairies in what is now central Saskatchewan — probably the Thickwood Hills. There he met the Naywatamee Poets before returning to York Factory in 1692.

At first, little came of Kelsey's journey. The Naywatamee Poets, whoever they were, never reached York Factory to trade, and prior to 1713 few other non-Cree and non-Assiniboine peoples from the plains and parklands regions did either. Nevertheless, the HBC officials had a good sense of the route inland from York Factory to Lake Winnipeg. They knew that this was potentially a rich source of furs and provisions, but they also knew that establishing posts inland from

Hudson Bay would not be easy or inexpensive.

Based on this knowledge, the Hudson's Bay Company pursued a very different approach to trade. It chose not to oppose the French directly by building posts in the interior. Instead, the HBC relied on Ojibwa, Cree, and Assiniboine middleman traders to acquire furs and then transport them to posts on Hudson Bay and James Bay. Indirectly, through these Aboriginal traders, a post such as York Factory could extend its trading hinterland to the foothills of the Rockies without facing the huge labour and transportation costs of the French fur trade. The HBC sought profit not so much in expanding trade as in carefully controlling the costs of production and seeking to maximize the returns on those furs it did acquire.

Overall, the fur trade in the early 18th century was shaped by limited demand. There was a significant, but largely finite, market for furs in Europe. European traders also learned that most Aboriginal groups had limited needs for European goods. A hunter might appreciate owning a metal knife, but convincing that same hunter to purchase a second knife, or two or three knives for different purposes, was difficult. Over the 18th century, a succession of the Hudson's Bay Company employees noted that contrary to established economic wisdom, lowering the price of trade goods would result in fewer furs being traded, not more. If Aboriginal traders could acquire the limited range of goods they needed with fewer furs, then they would simply spend less time trapping.

This observation suggests that trading with Europeans was not a critical consideration for most First Nations groups at this time. The Hudson's Bay Company kept careful records of the size of the trading parties that visited its posts. In the 1730s, on average, about 400 canoes a year visited York Factory and Churchill to trade. Since these canoes required crews of about two men, it is likely that fewer than a thousand people were travelling from inland to trade directly at these posts.

Admittedly, both posts also traded with significant num-

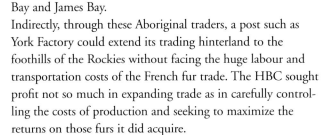

Gorgets traded by the English to the Native peoples, circa 1750.

bers of other people — like the Homeguard Indians who lived in the immediate area of the posts — and many of those coming in to trade from the interior were middleman traders themselves. As a result, these posts were collecting furs directly and indirectly from a much larger population. Nonetheless, trade records from the Hudson's Bay Company do not support the view that trade with Europeans was a central concern for most First Nations at this time. A few individuals may have chosen to trade at the bayside posts on a regular basis, and a larger group probably visited the posts on occasion. Nevertheless, a high proportion of people, even Cree and Assiniboine, probably visited a Hudson's Bay Company post only once or twice in their lifetimes, if at all.

Because of this limited trade potential, the Hudson's Bay Company put considerable effort into trying to find other trade "commodyties besides furs," as one company official put it. A major expense for the HBC was the need to send ships annually to its posts with cargoes of bulky trade goods. The return cargo of furs was valuable, but light and far from bulky. New products could easily be added on these return voyages. As a result, the HBC tried to develop a whaling operation at Churchill and to acquire oil from Inuit hunters in addition to furs. A senior company official, James Knight, organized an expedition to find the long-rumoured copper deposits of the Coppermine River area by sailing north from Churchill in 1719. Knight and all of his crew died at Marble Island off the northern coast of Hudson Bay, which limited interest in mining ventures for some time. Nonetheless, the HBC experimented with exporting Labrador Tea as a possible herbal remedy, and quills, feathers, deer horn, and other products as a way of supplementing the fur trade.

None of these products substantially changed the Hudson's Bay Company's operations. It did not become a mining company or whaling concern, nor did Labrador Tea replace more conventional teas in the British market. Still, the company was always willing to consider developing new busi-

Prince of Wales Fort.

ness interests, and the company's trade was never limited to just hides and furs.

Where the Hudson's Bay Company did have more success was in operating its posts with greater efficiency. Posts such as York Factory, Moose Factory, Fort Albany, and Churchill (also known as Prince of Wales Fort) were more than just trade sites. First of all, the men stationed at these posts were expected to work to provide for their own subsistence. Probably the single most important job undertaken by the HBC employees was cutting firewood to heat the post and timber to construct and repair it.

At Prince of Wales Fort, which was built after 1731 using stone, cutting timber for building was not a major issue. However, the stone buildings at Churchill were miserably cold, as stone is not a good insulator and Churchill's winters are notoriously severe. The fort consumed staggering quantities of firewood as a result. Employees hung heated cannon balls in the fort windows to retain some of the heat that otherwise just went straight up fireplace chimneys. The period from the late 17th to the mid-19th century is known as the Little Ice Age, and brutally long and cold winters were a feature of life at posts on Hudson Bay in these years.

Company employees were expected to provide as much of their own food as possible without relying on expensive, and often rather dubious, imported foods. The company expected its employees to maintain vegetable gardens, to keep livestock, and to hunt and fish to support themselves. Over the years company employees became more and more adept at these provisioning activities, although at most posts the bulk of the locally obtained "country" provisions — geese, ducks, caribou, moose, deer, and fish — were provided by the local Aboriginal populations.

The Hudson's Bay Company posts were organized by ranks. Each had an officer in charge and a number of other clerks, or "writers," who were viewed as "gentlemen" and allowed to dine in an officers' mess. Larger posts, such as York Factory and Churchill, might also have a sloop captain and a surgeon, who also claimed the status of gentlemen. However, most employees were grouped together as the "men," or company "servants." This larger group included tradesmen of various sorts, including blacksmiths, tinsmiths, coopers, tailors, masons, carpenters, and armourers. Others were classified — and paid — as fishermen and sailors. The largest group of employees was listed as "labourers." With no specific job skills, they might be required to work at any task around the post.

At Prince of Wales Fort in the early 18th century, the officer in charge, who was sometimes titled the "factor," or "governor," might earn £100 a year. Senior clerks, sloop captains, and surgeons were paid about £40 per annum, while an apprentice clerk might receive just £15. Skilled tradesmen were paid between £20 and £36 a year, while ordinary labourers were hired at £6 a year. This pay rose in 40s annual increments to £14 after five years of service. All employees were given room and board, even if most had to build that room and hunt for that board themselves.

As a result, the Hudson's Bay Company employees were reasonably, if not lavishly, paid. They could usually save at least some portion of their wages if they chose. In Britain, wages for tradesmen and labourers rarely offered much margin over living expenses, so service with the HBC had a certain appeal. James Isham, a company officer and thus perhaps slightly biased, claimed that a man earning 9s a week in Britain was lucky to save a few pence a year, whereas the HBC labourer might save £4 out of a salary of just £6. He went on to state that "It is not the pleasantness of the Country that makes men prefer itt [*sic*] to all other places, but the Ease, pleasure, and in truth the profitt [*sic*] they Gain by thier Sallery &c."

This was particularly true among residents of the Orkney Islands, who made up much of the company's workforce in the 18th century. The company's annual supply ships put in

Prince of Wales Fort.

for water and food at Stromness on the Orkney Islands as a last stop before crossing the North Atlantic. The company saw Orkneymen as hard working, reliable, frugal, and tolerant of the hard conditions found at posts located on Hudson Bay. For their part, Orkneymen were attracted by the wages the Hudson's Bay Company offered and the opportunity to save a portion of those wages. Work with the HBC was not as risky as joining the Royal Navy or whaling, and it did not require leaving the Orkneys forever as immigration to America might. Hired for a fixed contract term, a tradesman or labourer from the Orkneys could aspire to returning home in five years with enough savings to establish themselves in trade or on a small farm.

Joseph Robson, who had helped build Prince of Wales Fort and in the process became an implacable critic of the Hudson's Bay Company, famously characterized the policy of the company in the mid-18th century as a long sleep "at the edge of a frozen sea." Although Robson meant no compliment, the policy made sense in economic terms for a very long time. In many ways, the French and the HBC fur trades could be seen as complementary rather than directly competitive in the early 1700s.

Senior HBC officers and their families enjoyed more luxurious accommodations than the men, as this photograph of the "Big House" at Fort Edmonton in 1871 indicates.

However, two factors came together to challenge the Hudson's Bay Company's somnambulant approach to trade. The posts located on James Bay had long faced declining trade due to French activity inland, but for the most part, trade at York Factory and Churchill compensated for reduced trade in other areas. The HBC continued to produce enough furs to meet demand in Britain. However, by the 1740s, French traders had effectively encircled the main the HBC posts. Volumes of trade dropped significantly at all posts on James Bay and the western coast of Hudson Bay, and the costs of acquiring furs rose sharply. By the 1750s, the HBC was in economic trouble.

It was also under political attack in Britain for its lack of ambition in promoting the exploration, settlement, and expansion of trade alluded to under its charter. Led by Arthur Dobbs, a respected historian, economist, and armchair theorist of Arctic exploration, the charter rights of the Hudson's Bay Company were challenged. Dobbs was particularly opposed to the HBC's monopoly trade privileges, especially given the lukewarm support it offered in the search for a North West Passage. Dobbs published books and pamphlets arguing that the HBC charter should be revoked and that trade, settlement, and exploration would all be advanced if the fur trade were thrown open to competition. He also sponsored an expedition to search for the North West Passage in 1746. The main product of all of Dobbs's activity, however, was that in 1749 the British Parliament established a committee to enquire into "the state of the countries adjoining to Hudson Bay and of the trade carried on there."

This Parliamentary Committee took evidence from company officials and employees, and also from a number of prominent opponents of the Hudson's Bay Company, such as Dobbs and Robson. In the end the company's charter was reaffirmed, but not before a lot of damaging and sometimes scurrilous material was presented. The committee reported that there was little advantage in forcing the HBC to build posts inland as long as the French were well established there. Still, the company was made to look singularly unenterprising and complacent. It could do better.

The Hudson's Bay Company tried to respond. In 1754 it sent Anthony Henday inland from York Factory with a party of Cree led by a noted middleman trader named Attickasish,

or "The Little Deer." Henday was supposed to meet with the Archithinue and other Plains peoples to encourage them to visit York Factory to trade. Henday travelled more or less along the same route as Kelsey had to the Saskatchewan River and then west to the Battle River area. There he met a large camp of Archithinue, probably near what is now Red Deer, Alberta. Henday's journey is the first recorded visit to what is now Alberta by a European fur trader, although it is very likely French traders preceded him. His journal also makes it clear that Cree and Assiniboine traders regularly visited these people.

Historians and anthropologists remain unsure of exactly who Henday's Archithinue were. They may have been any of the major Plains peoples except for the Cree and Assiniboine, but most assume that he met a group of Blackfoot, or at least a Blackfoot-speaking people such as the Piegan or Blood/Kainai. Whoever they were, Henday was singularly unsuccessful in convincing them to visit York Factory to trade. The Archithinue informed Henday that they had no desire to make such a trip. They were well served by middleman traders such as Attickasish and by the French traders Henday met several times on his travels. Even more significantly, the Archithinue claimed to prefer travel by horse to canoes, and as result they had no interest in or need to make a long and dangerous journey to Hudson Bay just to trade with Europeans.

It is impossible to know how the Hudson's Bay Company would have responded had international events not intervened. In 1755 the long-simmering conflict between American colonists and New France flared into open warfare in the Ohio River area. By 1756 a full-scale colonial war had broken out. Britain made a concerted effort to capture New France, and by the late 1750s, French traders were abandoning their posts in the far North West. As every Canadian student knows, General Wolfe captured Quebec in 1759, and the last vestiges of French military resistance in Quebec ended in 1760. In the trading vacuum, the HBC posts saw sudden increases in their trade, reversing the trends of the previous two decades. The Hudson's Bay Company could return to its "sleepy" trade approach and await the implications of the treaty of 1763 that ended the Seven Years' War.

5

"A Mari Usque Ad Mare" — The Fur Trade, 1763–1800

The British army that captured Quebec in 1759 also sent shock waves through the fur trade. Eighteenth-century armies always travelled with a supporting cast of merchants, small traders, and other service providers in their trains. Wolfe's forces were no exception, and after 1759 growing numbers of Anglo-American merchants found their way into the newly conquered territories. The fur trade represented one potential area of profitable business, especially as the Seven Years' War had disrupted the old fur trade system of New France.

The first obvious manifestation of this change was the outbreak of Pontiac's War in the Great Lakes region. The causes of this struggle are numerous and complex. Historian Olive Dickason has argued that Pontiac, a leader of the Ottawas, and his many supporters represent "an early manifestation of nativistic movements by which Amerindians sought to cope with the invasion of their lands and missionary pressures against their way of life." Certainly the failure of Britain to keep land-hungry settlers from encroaching on the lands of the Ottawas and other First Nations was one of the initial causes of this war. So too were the uncertainties created by changes in the fur trade and feeling on the part of many Anglo-Americans that the defeat of New France also implied

Pontiac taking up the war hatchet in 1763.

the defeat of New France's Aboriginal allies. Obviously it did not.

In 1762, Pontiac and Neolin, a Delaware prophet who urged his supporters to cut off all connections with the British, started to build a broad movement of different First Nations to resist the British. The goal was to push the British out of their forts and trading posts throughout the Great Lakes region, along with the settlers who followed in the wake of the fur trade. By the early summer of 1763, nine British forts in the Great Lakes area had been captured and Fort Detroit was under siege. The most famous of these battles was the capture of Fort Michilimackinac, a key fort and fur trade post located on the strait connecting Lake Huron with Lake Michigan. Under the guise of playing a lacrosse game, Pontiac's supporters gained entrance to the fort and overwhelmed its garrison.

By the winter of 1763–64, the British military presence in the Great Lakes and west of the Appalachian Mountains was effectively reduced to just Detroit, Fort Niagara, and Fort Pitt (on the Ohio River at modern Pittsburgh). Over the winter, however, the resistance faltered, and in 1764 a peace conference with 19 First Nations was held at Fort Niagara. One by one different First Nations abandoned the cause, and Pontiac was left isolated. Still, it was not until 1766 that a final peace was negotiated.

In the interim, the British negotiated a final peace treaty with France, in which France agreed to give up Quebec to Britain and Louisiana to Spain. Britain was then faced with the issue of what to do with its new colony of Quebec. The Proclamation of 1763 was intended to settle the question of Quebec's future and the unrest that led to Pontiac's War. In theory, the Proclamation closed the interior to new Anglo-American settlement. Part of the plan was to divert new settlement north to the St. Lawrence Valley, which at a stroke would mollify First Nations in the interior and help to make Quebec less French. In reality, few American colonists moved north, and pressure on western lands continued. Fur traders based in Albany and Schenectady in New York in particular expanded their operations in the new territories south of the Great Lakes. Still, the small English-speaking population of Quebec was augmented, and many found their way into the fur trade.

Fur traders had to develop ties with British merchant houses to secure credit for the purchase of trade goods and to market the furs acquired through trade. This arrangement gave Anglo-American traders a significant advantage, since many already had these kinds of business connections. French-speaking fur traders also had to adjust to the new situation. If they were wealthy enough, some left the fur trade, and even New France, altogether. Others tried to find a place in the trade based on their knowledge and experience.

It was once believed that the end of New France meant

An Ottawa pouch and knife with sheath from the 18th century.

the effective end of Canadien control of the fur trade. Newer research suggests the story is more complicated than that. Some French-speaking merchants did re-establish themselves in the fur trade, often in partnership with the new Anglo-American merchants moving into Montreal and, to a lesser extent, Quebec City. Members of the Baby family, for example, had considerable success repositioning themselves as leading figures in the Great Lakes fur trade after 1763. Large Montreal-based fur trade companies often included some French-speaking owners and senior officials. However, after 1763, to be French-speaking meant more and more to be a company employee and not an owner.

The defeat of New France also gave the Hudson's Bay Company an unexpected period of respite as new Montreal-based fur trade companies gradually established themselves. The old fur trade of New France was never totally abandoned — a few traders remained inland above Lake Superior through this troubled period — but essentially the infrastructure of the inland posts, the sources of food supplies, and a canoe brigade system linking Montreal with posts on the Saskatchewan River had to be restored following the Seven Years' War and Pontiac's War.

This activity enabled the Hudson's Bay Company to put off any serious consideration of building a system of inland posts supplied from Hudson Bay. However, the company did continue to send employees inland in the hope of attracting more, and new, Aboriginal groups down to its posts on Hudson Bay and James Bay. Samuel Hearne undertook the most notable and ambitious of these inland journeys from Prince of Wales Fort in the years 1770–72.

Prince of Wales Fort at Churchill had always been an anomaly in the Hudson's Bay Company trading system, and not just because it was built as a stone fortification. It was located well to the north of other posts, near the edge of the boreal forest and taiga regions. It was used as the base for the HBC's modest attempts to establish a whaling industry, and from Churchill the company sent sloops, or small sailing vessels, north to trade with Inuit and Chipewyan groups along the Hudson Bay coast. These sloop voyages had clearly shown that there was no North West Passage to be found in Hudson Bay, and no copper mines either — despite some wishful thinking on the part of James Knight and others.

Churchill attracted trade from a Homeguard Cree population living in the Hudson Bay Lowland region, but much of its trade in the 18th century came from groups of Chipewyan who travelled down to the post from their territories far inland. These "trading" Chipewyan did not usually use canoes, except to cross rivers. Most rivers in the far north are unsuitable for canoe travel because they are shallow and often have strong currents. Instead, the Chipewyan who visited Churchill travelled hundreds of kilometres overland, laboriously carrying their furs or pulling them on toboggans.

Hearne was sent inland to do two main things. He was asked to discover, if possible, the source of the copper that was brought in to company

Samuel Hearne.

posts from time to time. He was also supposed to encourage more Chipewyan and other Athapaskan peoples to visit Churchill to trade. After two false starts in 1769 and early 1770, Hearne left Prince of Wales Fort in December 1770 with a remarkable leader of the "trading" Chipewyan, named Matonabbee. Matonabbee agreed to guide Hearne inland to the Coppermine River, but Hearne would have to travel according to the pace and interests of Matonabbee and his supporters. As a result, Hearne's journal provides a detailed account of the lives of those Chipewyan, who chose to make the fur trade a central part of their economy.

Matonabbee led Hearne on a meandering course inland, more or less following the edge of the boreal forest. To modern readers, this circuitous journey in the depths of winter might seem foolish, but in winter frozen rivers and lakes provided no real obstacle to overland travel. Matonabbee pointed out that travelling directly to the Coppermine River was the real folly, since in winter it was far

A North West View of Prince of Wales' Fort in Hudson's Bay, North America, painting by Samuel Hearne, 1777.

Bloody Fall, Coppermine River, George Back, 1822.

better to avoid the Barrens and wait until the caribou herds returned there in spring. As Hearne travelled inland, he realized that most of the Chipewyan rarely, if ever, visited posts to trade, preferring to sell their furs to people like Matonabbee in return for the limited range of European trade goods they needed. In fact, Matonabbee was not just trading with fellow Chipewyan but also with the Dogribs and other Athapaskan groups.

Hearne also came to question the value of the fur trade for groups such as the Chipewyan. At Wholdiah Lake he met with a band who had constructed a large deer hedge, a fence that allowed them to funnel migrating caribou — or "deer" as fur traders called them — into snares and narrow openings. This technique made hunting caribou much more efficient and reliable. As Hearne observed, the Chipewyan living near the deer hedge lived comfortably, but they produced few furs. As a result, they owned few European goods, and Hearne saw

no evidence that their lives were any poorer for this:

> The real wants of these people are few, and easily supplied…those who endeavour to possess more, are always the most unhappy, and may, in fact, be said to be only slaves and carriers to the rest…. It is true the carriers pride themselves much on the respect which is shewn them at the factory; to obtain which they frequently run great risques of being starved to death….

Hearne went on to note that the Chipewyan who did not visit Churchill to trade on a regular basis "…live generally in a state of plenty, without trouble or risque; and consequently must be the most happy, and, in truth, the most independent also."

In May 1771, Matonabbee and his supporters finally started out onto the Barrens. Hearne was forced to reflect on his real position in the expedition when he realized that Matonabbee and the other Chipewyan were less concerned with showing him copper deposits than with attacking the Inuit who lived on the Coppermine River. Hearne's account of a one-sided battle with the Inuit — apparently embellished for effect by Hearne's editor and publisher — is well known and much quoted, but it adds little to our knowledge of the fur trade. What does matter is that Hearne saw the mouth of the Coppermine River and realized that it had little value to European navigators. The river mouth was choked with ice in July and marked by rapids and waterfalls. It was barely usable by canoes. The much-sought-after copper mines did not impress Hearne either. He found one large piece of almost pure copper after a search of some hours but concluded that mining the site was not a commercial proposition. All that remained was the long, long walk home to Churchill, which Hearne reached on June 29, 1772.

It was an epic journey by two very interesting people — Samuel Hearne and Matonabbee — but it resulted in no new trade and was a disappointing conclusion to decades of speculation about valuable mines that existed just beyond the reach of European traders. In fact, within a decade the middleman trade that brought Matonabbee and Hearne together was effectively at an end. Hearne's journey was not the start of something new; it was more the last gasp of the old Hudson's Bay Company trading system.

As early as 1767 — just four years after Quebec had been ceded to the British — Montreal-based traders had re-established trade connections through Michilimackinac, Kaministiquia, and Grande Portage with the Lake Winnipeg, Red River, and lower Saskatchewan River areas. Canoes were sent out with trade goods to Fort Dauphin, Fort La Reine, and Fort La Prairie (Portage la Prairie). A Mr. Findlay is even supposed to have reached the Fort La Corne area, perhaps as early as 1767. These traders adopted the methods pioneered by the de la Vérendryes and quickly became as much of a threat to the Hudson's Bay Company as their French predecessors.

By 1771–72 these new pedlars were well enough established at key sites such as Cedar Lake, The Pas, and on the Saskatchewan River that fur returns at York Factory dropped sharply once again, just as they had declined at posts on James Bay such as Moose Factory and Albany. The Hudson's

Bay Company sent Matthew Cocking inland in 1772 to try to assess the situation, and Cocking's journal makes it clear that there was no easy solution this time. He noted several times that inland groups had no desire to make the journey to York Factory when they could get what they required from Aboriginal middlemen or from the Montreal pedlars.

After just over a century of basing their trade on posts located on Hudson Bay and James Bay, the Hudson's Bay Company decided in 1774 that it had no choice but to try to compete directly with Montreal traders in the interior. Samuel Hearne, the experienced Arctic traveller, was charged with

Kakabeka Falls, by George Back, 1825.

building a post at Cumberland House in what is now northern Saskatchewan. Located on Cumberland Lake along the Saskatchewan River, this post was intended to recapture at least some of the trade that was going increasingly to the pedlars. It had some success in this regard, and the HBC gradually increased the number of inland posts it operated; for example, Hudson House was built near what is now Prince Albert in 1776. However, the HBC found supplying these inland posts very difficult and expensive.

The Hudson's Bay Company had few employees with any experience living inland or skill with canoes, unlike the Montreal traders, who could call on a ready workforce with decades of experience in these areas. No less importantly, there was no birch bark in the Hudson Bay lowlands area, so the HBC initially had to rely on canoes that it bought from Aboriginal traders. Until the company developed its own system of inland transportation based on wooden York boats in the 1790s, it remained at a real disadvantage in competition with Montreal traders.

Of course, the traders from Montreal faced their own particular transportation issues. As the de la

Samuel Hearne etched his name on a rock in Sloop's Cove in 1767.

Vérendryes had found, supplying posts so far from Montreal required considerable organization and a complex transportation system. The system that developed was based on using large canoes, the *canot du maître,* to take trade goods to interior depots at the western end of Lake Superior. There the Montreal-based canoe brigades met the men coming down from interior posts in smaller canoes, the *canot du nord.* These "north" canoes suited travel on the smaller rivers and lakes of the interior. They needed smaller crews — just four to six men instead of the eight to ten needed for a *canot du maître* — and they were much easier to portage. A *canot du maître* carried a cargo of about 60 packs of freight, each pack weighing roughly 40 kilograms, or 90 pounds. In total, these canoes carried about 2.5 tonnes of goods along with food, supplies, and a crew that added about another 1.5 tonnes of weight. By contrast, the smaller *canot du nord* could carry about 20 to 25 packs of trade goods and about 10 packs of

food, supplies, and baggage — about half the cargo capacity of a *canot du maître.*

Grande Portage emerged as the main inland depot and rendezvous point for pedlars and men from the interior posts. There they met and exchanged cargoes, with the furs returning to Montreal and trade goods being transported inland to wintering posts. This system required both business coordination and access to capital and credit, since the return on stocks of trade goods might not be realized for several years. It was also a risky business, since most of the early companies were relatively small, trading at just one or two interior posts and bringing in cargoes of just a few canoes. Surviving trade licences for 1778 indicate that most inland trading ventures consisted of fewer 6 canoes. The largest, backed by John McGill and Thomas Frobisher, was just 12 canoes. Consequently, the loss of a single canoe or poor trade at a given post could have a major financial impact on such small operations.

To minimize risk and to make the complex logistics of this long-distance trade work effectively, Montreal trading interests began to merge into larger and larger partnerships. This tendency towards consolidation in the "North West" trade can be seen in an agreement reached in 1779 and formalized in 1780. The agreement noted that in 1779, licences were granted too late in the year to forward goods to posts in the North West. As a result, the main companies engaged in this trade "joined their stock together and made one common interest of the whole." The venture then assigned 16 shares to nine different trading companies based on the value of the goods they shipped inland. This model worked so well it was continued in subsequent years, although the companies and individuals involved did change from time to time, and not all the North West trading interests participated.

By 1783–84, the main partnership, known as the North West Company, was in place. It was dominated by brothers Benjamin and Joseph Frobisher and Simon McTavish, and it claimed a trade of about £100,000 a year. This was a considerable sum at the time, although the company absorbed high labour and other costs. Most of the traders not included in the North West Company formed a parallel group known as Gregory McLeod and Company, which competed strenuously with the North West Company until merging with it in 1787. The new company, which kept the name the North West Company, dominated the Canadian fur trade in the North West for the rest of the century.

The partnership that would become the North West Company pursued a particularly aggressive and expansionary trading policy, based initially on the work of Peter Pond, a colourful and controversial character. In 1778, Pond was chosen by fellow traders to take a supply of trade goods over perhaps the most famous of fur trade portages: Portage la Loche, or Methy Portage. This route traversed the height of land separating the Churchill River system from the Clearwater River. This also separated the Hudson Bay drainage system from the Arctic Ocean system. The route had been described to Canadian traders and was used regularly by Aboriginal travellers bringing furs from the rich Athabasca area to posts on the Churchill River, but Pond showed how it could be used to extend direct trade contact into a new and very important region.

This most gruelling of portages — it is about 20 kilometres, or 13 miles, long — was key to the Montreal-based fur trade for both practical and symbolic reasons. Although the North West Company and other companies never conceded the legal validity of the Hudson's Bay Company's charter, trading beyond Portage La Loche meant that the Montreal traders had reached beyond the area covered in King Charles's expansive gift to the HBC. Even more important, it allowed the pedlars to intercept the supply of furs that had formerly been taken down to Prince of Wales Fort by Matonabbee and the other trading Chipewyan. In providing direct trade contact with the Aboriginal population of the entire Athabasca region, it quickly proved to be the source of most of the North West Company's furs. So rich was the area

that the Athabasca region came to be known as the Eldorado of the fur trade.

Certainly the immediate returns for Pond and his backers were immense. After crossing Portage La Loche, Pond travelled down the Clearwater River to the Athabasca River before building a post on the Athabasca River somewhere between what is now Fort McMurray and Lake Athabasca. Alexander Mackenzie, a colleague of Pond's, later wrote that Pond was able to trade directly with the "vast concourse of the Knisteneaux [Cree] and Chepewyan tribes, who used to carry their furs annually to Churchill." Saved from the labour and risk of this journey, they "were immediately reconciled to give an advanced price for the articles necessary to their comfort and convenience. Mr. Pond's reception and success was accordingly beyond his expectation; and he procured twice as many furs as his canoes could carry."

Pond's discovery really was the beginning of the end for the trade connection between the Hudson's Bay Company's posts on Hudson Bay and Indian middleman traders, such as Matonabbee. There was no need for Chipewyan and other Athapaskan groups to transport furs overland to Churchill any longer, and by 1782 these trade ties were completely broken.

The seeds of this change were sown not in London or

Fort Prince of Wales, 1995.

This painting by Peter Rindisbacher shows how York Boats had to be "tracked," or literally pulled, inland against the current by their crews.

York Factory but in Montreal and the American colonies. One of the consequences of the American Revolution for the fur trade was that after the peace agreement of 1783, the old "South West" fur trade became American territory. Major posts such as Detroit and Michilimackinac were no longer part of British territory. Some years later, in 1803, it was also realized that Grande Portage was on American territory and the North West Company had to move its inland depot to the old French trading location of Kaministiquia, now known as Fort William. The southern trade did not immediately pass into American hands, but after 1783 the Montreal fur trade was increasingly focused on the northwest, and the Athabasca district in particular. The arrival of thousands of Loyalist refugees in Canada ensured a growing pool of tough and talented potential employees for companies such as the North West Company, and in the ensuing years Loyalists and the

children of Loyalists played crucial roles in the Canadian fur trade.

The American Revolution also struck a blow at the fortunes of the Hudson's Bay Company through one of the least-known military engagements of Canadian history. In 1782 the French sent a naval squadron of three ships to Hudson Bay as part of France's support for the American revolutionaries. The plan was to disrupt the trade of the HBC, and it succeeded to a remarkable degree. A noted officer and explorer, Jean-François de Galaup, Comte de la Pérouse, commanded the French force. Despite having no charts of Hudson Bay or crews with experience sailing in Arctic waters, de la Pérouse managed to reach Hudson Bay and anchored off Prince of Wales Fort on August 8, 1782.

Samuel Hearne, who had returned to Churchill to take command of the Hudson's Bay Company post there, made some modest attempts to defend Prince of Wales Fort. Cannons were loaded, but only 39 men were stationed at Churchill and they were scarcely trained artillerymen. Hearne had served with the Royal Navy and he quickly realized, when de la Pérouse landed several hundred soldiers the following day, that resistance was futile. He surrendered the fort without a shot being fired.

In later years, others criticized Hearne for his pusillanimous approach, although the Hudson's Bay Company itself appears to have understood that Hearne had no choice. The reality was that Prince of Wales Fort, despite its cannons and seemingly imposing 12-metre-wide (40-foot-wide) walls, was a military white elephant. Joseph Robson, the author and mason who had helped build the fort, claimed that the fort's walls would collapse at the first or second discharge, and de la Pérouse stated that just one of his ships would have reduced the fort to rubble in short order.

Still, in this inglorious fashion, the main the Hudson's Bay Company fortification on Hudson Bay was captured. De la Pérouse then ensured it would not be reused. He spiked the post's cannons and used the HBC's own stores of gunpowder to blow gaping holes in the walls, but not before seizing the post's stores of trade goods and furs. De la Pérouse also made Hearne and his men prisoners. He left supplies of gunpowder and shot behind for any people who might come in to trade and then left to attack York Factory. The officer in charge there, Humphrey Marten, tried to negotiate with the French, but the result was the same. York Factory too was surrendered, and by September 2, 1782, de la Pérouse and his forces were on their way home. It was later estimated that this expedition cost the HBC over £14,000 in losses, a financial setback the company could ill afford at a time of growing competition with its Montreal rivals. The raid also disrupted trade for many years. The HBC supply ship was unable to land at Churchill or York Factory, so inland posts such as Cumberland and Hudson House were left short of trade goods. This in turn meant that Aboriginal groups who traded with the HBC were left without supplies for a year. For the trading Chipewyan, this was a serious blow. Although a post was re-established at Churchill in 1783, as well as at York Factory, Fort Churchill never attracted trade from Athapaskan groups in the Lake Athabasca area again. They traded at local

posts thereafter, and Churchill just served the population of Cree, Chipewyan, and Inuit who settled in the area along the Hudson Bay coast.

It was later reported that Matonabbee, having heard Prince of Wales Fort was captured and destroyed, hanged himself, knowing that his position as a trading leader and mediator between the English traders and his fellow Chipewyans was over. It was also reported that six of his wives and several children starved to death without Matonabbee or the Hudson's Bay Company there to help support them. Untold numbers of other Chipewyan and Homeguard Cree faced serious privation and even death because of the disruption in the fur trade produced by this odd and almost unknown campaign in the American War of Independence.

Part of the reason this story is so little known is that it occurred at almost exactly the same time as one of the most important events in the history of western Canada. Just prior to the arrival of the French forces at York Factory, several Indians arrived from the interior obviously suffering from smallpox. Humphrey Marten immediately took steps to try to keep them from contacting the local Homeguard Cree population, but within days several people had died near the post. Because the French attack interrupted daily entries in the post journal, we will never know if the smallpox spread to the local Cree as well. What we do know is that if the people living near York Factory were spared, they were part of a tiny minority across the length and breadth of the northwest.

The smallpox pandemic of 1781–82 was not the first such epidemic in the North West. The de la Vérendryes reported an outbreak of the disease over the years 1736–37, but there were so few Europeans and trading posts in the interior that the scale of this epidemic and its mortality rate remain unknown. By 1781–82, however, the horrifying consequences of the disease are well documented. The disease was introduced from the Missouri River area and spread with discouraging rapidity across the plains and parklands and into the boreal forest region. There, lower population densities and a more scattered population helped to limit the further spread of infection. Nevertheless, almost all of what we now think of as the Prairie Provinces and the Northwest Territories were affected, and the disease may well have spread still further without it being recorded.

A Cree elder living among the Peigan would later tell David Thompson how smallpox reached the plains. Saukamappee explained that the Peigan came on a camp of some enemies — possibly Shoshone — and found them all dead or dying in their tents. The Peigan had no sense, however, that they could catch a disease from others "any more than a wounded Man could give his wound to another." They plundered the camp, and within days they too were dying from smallpox. Fleeing north, they inadvertently spread

were staggering. Samuel Hearne estimated that among the Chipewyans who formerly traded at Churchill, as many as nine out of ten died. Most estimates of mortality were lower, but some contemporary observers did suggest that perhaps one in two Plains Indians died. Mitchell Oman, a Hudson's Bay Company officer at Hudson House, stated that when he returned to the post there was no "crowd of Indians to welcome us," just "solitary silence." Knowing what this meant, Oman said, "our hearts failed us." The disease hit children and older people particularly hard, wiping out the knowledge of elders and the hope represented by young people at a stroke. Small wonder that Saukamappee told Thompson the disease shook individuals' faith and made them think "the Good Spirit had forsaken us and allowed the Bad Spirit to become our Master." As he succinctly stated, "we shall never be again the same people."

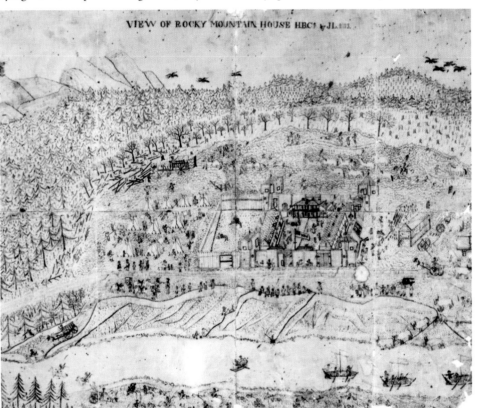

VIEW OF ROCKY MOUNTAIN HOUSE HBC? by JL.1873.

Rocky Mountain House was established in 1799 and rebuilt several times. This illustration by Jean L'Heureux shows the last Rocky Mountain House as it appeared in 1873.

the disease to new victims, and so the disease spread from band to band across the northwest. People travelling to posts to trade were a particularly dangerous source of new infections, and so the fur trade inadvertently made the epidemic worse.

Smallpox changed everything. Reported mortality rates

Aboriginal societies were extremely resilient, and in time they recovered enough to begin trading again. After 1782, however, the fur trade changed dramatically. For example, in the Red River area the former Cree and Assiniboine population was sharply reduced. Groups of Ojibwa known as the Saulteaux, because they came originally from the Sault Ste. Marie area, moved into this important fur trade region. Further north, some Swampy Cree groups relocated south and west, away from their traditional lands in the Hudson Bay Lowland area. Right across western Canada, significant population movements took place in the wake of the smallpox epidemic.

The European fur traders were not immune to this demographic change either. Because most fur trade employees had been exposed previously to smallpox and had some immunity to the disease, few were directly affected by the epidemic. Many, however, had married into First Nations communities and thus lost immediate family members, relatives, friends, and customers. The loss of population also undermined earlier middleman trade networks. Just as the French had had to go out to trade directly with interior groups after the trade network of the Hurons collapsed in the 1640s, in the 1780s and 1790s traders from Montreal and Hudson Bay moved further inland, opening direct trade with groups who had previously used Cree, Assiniboine, and Chipewyan middleman traders as their sources of European trade goods.

This expansion can easily be traced by posts located on the North Saskatchewan River. In 1782, the North West and the Hudson's Bay Companies had not really pushed direct trade much beyond Fort Corne and the junction of the North and South Saskatchewan rivers. This area had had posts since the de la Verendryes, but there had been no real effort to reproduce the experiment of Fort Jonquière and push direct trade towards the Rockies. Nor is it likely that Cree and Assiniboine middlemen would have encouraged such a move, but after 1782 these conditions had changed.

By the early 1790s, both companies began construction of posts on the North Saskatchewan River. The North West Company built Fort George near what is now Elk Point, Alberta, in 1792, and the Hudson's Bay Company followed suit with Buckingham House, built almost side by side with Fort George. So close were the posts that one resident described the two companies' employees as both opponents and neighbours. Edmonton House (HBC) and Fort Augustus (NWC) were established in 1795, and in 1799 Acton House (HBC) and Rocky Mountain House (NWC) carried direct trade between European traders and Aboriginal groups to the foothills of the Rockies.

The North Saskatchewan posts took advantage of the river's location near the edge of the plains and parklands regions. North of the river was good fur country. Around Edmonton House it was claimed that beaver and otter were so common, "Women and Children kill them with sticks and hatchets." The plains to the south produced fewer furs —

mostly wolf — but lots of provisions in the form of fresh and dried buffalo meat and pemmican, which quickly became the preferred food of the canoe brigades.

A half-kilogram of pemmican was considered a replacement for up to 2 kilograms of fresh meat, and canoemen were given a ration of just under 1 kilogram of pemmican a day. They needed this sort of massive calorie intake to paddle, portage, and track canoes hour after hour, day after day. As a result, fur trade companies required staggering quantities of pemmican. In 1806 the North West Company sent 156 canoes inland from Fort William. Each canoe required between six and ten bags of pemmican, each weighing about 40 kilograms. The North West Company alone needed roughly 50 to 60 tonnes of pemmican a year. The Hudson's Bay Company required about a third of the North West Company's total.

As a result, pemmican had to be produced in near industrial quantities. Most was made by fur trade company employees and their families. Pemmican was rarely a trade item, although companies purchased large quantities of dried, pounded meat and fat to make it. Most pemmican came from the Saskatchewan, Assiniboine, and Red River posts. In the early 1790s, Fort George was expected to produce over 300 bags of pemmican a year — about 12 tonnes of it, which required the meat from hundreds of bison.

Not surprisingly, many of the North Saskatchewan River posts were moved several times. This movement may have had something to do with the impact posts had on local game populations. Some archaeologists have also speculated that within a few years the sheer volume of carcasses and debris from all that meat processing would have made them singularly unpleasant places to live and work.

The North Saskatchewan River posts also served many different peoples, including Cree and Assiniboine, Blackfoot, Peigan, Blood/Kainai, and Gros Ventre/Atsina. Given the numbers of different First Nations trading at these posts, they could be dangerous places, and to some extent new posts were built to try to keep different groups apart. Rocky Mountain and Acton Houses, for example, were built initially to serve the Peigan and to give them an alternative to trading at Fort Augustus and Edmonton House.

On the North Saskatchewan River the Hudson's Bay

Company tried to match the North West and other Montreal fur trade companies post for post, but only the Montreal traders had any real presence in the lands above Portage La Loche. Pond's initial work establishing a direct fur trade on the Athabasca River near Lake Athabasca had paid huge financial dividends. Based on reports he received from his trading partners, Pond speculated that the fur trade could be pushed to the Pacific Ocean from posts based in the Athabasca area. He theorized that the large river that flowed out of Great Slave Lake might empty into Cook Inlet, a large bay Captain Cook had seen on the north Pacific coast. Pond never got to act upon this idea, in part because his impetuous and irascible nature got him into trouble. He was implicated in the deaths of two fellow fur traders. Although he was never charged with any crime, a cloud of suspicion hung around him, and in 1788 he left the fur trade. Before doing so, however, he passed on many of his ideas about trade and exploration to his second-in-command at Fort Chipewyan on Lake Athabasca, Alexander Mackenzie.

The son of a Loyalist, Mackenzie moved to Montreal during the American War of Independence and soon found work in the fur trade. He was ambitious and remarkably able. Throughout his career Mackenzie was never content to be simply a successful trader and partner in fur trade companies. Instead, like Pond, he was something of a business visionary, planning ways to restructure and expand the fur trade into new regions and ventures. He presented many of these ideas in a book entitled *Voyages from Montreal through the continent of North America,* which combined an account of his explorations with one of the first serious attempts to write a history of the fur trade up to 1800.

In 1789, Mackenzie had the opportunity to test Pond's

Alexander MacKenzie.

theory. Mackenzie left Fort Chipewyan on Lake Athabasca and travelled north to Great Slave Lake, then continued along what is now known as Mackenzie River to the ocean. Unfortunately for Mackenzie and the North West Company, it was the Arctic and not the Pacific Ocean. Mackenzie reputedly called his discovery the River of Disappointment, but soon after his employers built a series of posts along its course stretching north almost to the Arctic Ocean.

Mackenzie may have been disappointed, but he was not defeated. He decided to explore westwards along the other major river flowing into Lake Athabasca, the Peace River. After wintering at Fort Fork, a post located near the current site of Peace River, Alberta, Mackenzie travelled along the Peace to its headwaters in the Rockies in 1793. From there he crossed the continental divide and reached the upper Fraser River. Following the advice of Aboriginal informants, he decided not to follow this notoriously difficult river and instead travelled overland to the Bella Coola River, which he used to reach the Pacific coast.

No posts were built in the years immediately following Mackenzie's second — less disappointing but equally epic — expedition, but he laid the groundwork for the Montreal-based fur trade to become a truly transcontinental enterprise after 1800. In less than 40 years, fur traders from Montreal had crossed the continent; forced the Hudson's Bay Company to completely change its trading system; recovered from the devastating impact of a smallpox epidemic; and figured out the logistics of how to move trade goods inland from Montreal to the Rocky Mountains and the edge of the Arctic Ocean, and furs out to markets in Europe, while still making substantial profits. This remains one of the greatest achievements in North American economic history.

6

Fur Trade Wars and the Creation of a New Hudson's Bay Company, 1800–1821

Alexander Mackenzie's voyages had shown that a true transcontinental fur trade was possible, but making it a practical proposition was another matter. The North West Company began establishing a network of trading posts on the Mackenzie River from 1800 onwards, but expansion west of the Rockies was more complicated.

Alexander Mackenzie left the North West Company in the late 1790s, and in 1800 he joined a rival partnership of Montreal traders that called itself the New North West Company. However, because it marked its bales of furs and trade goods with the symbol "XY," it was generally known as the XY Company in fur trade circles. The XY Company never became the vehicle for Mackenzie's great plans for a reorganized fur trade, but it competed vigorously with the North West Company. In a pattern that would repeat itself many times in the future, the NWC responded by buying out the XY Company in 1804. The main investors in the XY Company were offered 25 percent of the shares in a reorganized the NWC, and the most able of the XY Company's traders found positions with the NWC. Mackenzie retired to Scotland, but he remained an influential figure in fur trade circles whose ideas influenced the business strategies of the North West Company, Hudson's Bay Company, and American fur trade companies into the 1820s.

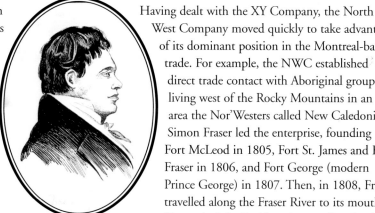

Simon Fraser.

Having dealt with the XY Company, the North West Company moved quickly to take advantage of its dominant position in the Montreal-based trade. For example, the NWC established direct trade contact with Aboriginal groups living west of the Rocky Mountains in an area the Nor'Westers called New Caledonia. Simon Fraser led the enterprise, founding Fort McLeod in 1805, Fort St. James and Fort Fraser in 1806, and Fort George (modern Prince George) in 1807. Then, in 1808, Fraser travelled along the Fraser River to its mouth. He reached the Pacific only to realize that he had not found either the Columbia or a very useful canoe route to reach the Pacific, but one of the least navigable of Canada's major rivers.

In fact, New Caledonia was always a bit of a disappointment to fur traders. It never became a particularly profitable trade district for the North West Company. It was known as something of a hardship posting, as food supplies were limited. Fur traders subsisted on a diet of salmon virtually year-round there, but the real issue was its remote location. The New Caledonia posts had to be supplied by a staggeringly long canoe route stretching all the way from Lake Superior inland to Fort Chipewyan on Lake Athabasca, and then west along the Peace River through the mountains into what is now northern British Columbia. In later years, the

Hudson's Bay Company tried supplying New Caledonia using a somewhat shorter, but still far from direct, route along the Athabasca River and through the Yellowhead Pass. Since Fort St. James is located over 4,000 kilometres (or about 2,600 miles) from York Factory, even this route was difficult to use and costly to maintain. By the mid-19th century, New Caledonia was usually supplied from Fort Vancouver and Fort Langley on the Pacific coast.

The North West Company had greater success on the Columbia River, but here too the story was not a simple one. Following the smallpox epidemic of the early 1780s, Blackfoot-speaking groups (the Blackfoot, or Siksika; Peigan; and Blood/Kainai), along with other allied peoples such as the Sarsi or T'suu Tina, emerged as the dominant First Nations in the plains and foothills regions between the North Saskatchewan and Missouri Rivers. Plains-dwelling peoples

Artist's impression of a Blackfoot encampment near the Rockies in the 19th century. Blackfoot-speaking peoples became increasingly involved in the fur trade when posts were built on the North Saskatchewan River in the 1790s and early 1800s.

had limited access to fur-bearing animals and mostly traded wolf skins before the development of a large buffalo-robe trade in the later 19th century. However, the Peigan, who lived in the foothills along the eastern slopes of the Rockies, had greater access to beaver and other fur-bearing animals. As a result, they took a particular interest in the fur trade, and the North West and Hudson's Bay companies built Rocky Mountain House and Acton House specifically to serve the trade interests of the Peigan.

The Peigan and other Blackfoot-speaking groups also maintained a middleman trade network with other southern bands who could not — or would not — visit posts on the North Saskatchewan River, and with peoples living west of the Rockies in what is now the British Columbia interior. Access to

An odd languid portrayal of traders by George Caleb Bingham, 1845.

trade goods gave the Blackfoot-speaking peoples a clear military advantage over their neighbours. This advantage did not always have to be exercised, but it did offer a certain sense of security. If hostilities arose, the Blackfoot, Bloods, and Peigan would be better armed than their opponents.

The American government's decision to send the Lewis and Clark expedition through the Missouri River region and into the Rockies threatened this situation, and in July 1806 a Blackfoot band confronted Lewis and Clark in what is now northern Montana. Lewis and Clark informed the Blackfoot party that the American government intended to open trade with the Shoshone, Nez Perce, and other peoples. The Blackfoot responded by trying to take Lewis and Clark's supply of trade guns to forestall this end, and in the ensuing struggle at least two Blackfoot were killed. These deaths confirmed the Blackfoot, Peigan, and Blood in their hostility towards American traders, and for roughly two decades, until 1831, they

Tsimshian man and HBC trader exchanging a handkerchief for an otter skin. The fur trade was always based on the different values people put on material goods.

managed to keep the Americans from establishing posts on the upper Missouri River.

Prior to the 1780s, the Kutenai Indians had apparently visited the plains on occasion to hunt bison, but by the early 1800s they had retreated to the interior plateau of what is now southern British Columbia. Nevertheless, small groups of Kutenai had contacted traders at Fort Edmonton and Rocky Mountain House to encourage Euro-Canadian traders to build posts west of the Rockies. The Kutenai hoped that this would ensure a regular supply of European goods and at the same time provide an alternative to trading with the Peigan. For their part, the Peigan opposed such a move, since it would have undermined their middleman trade and their position, along with the Blackfoot and Blood, as the strongest military force on the western plains.

The Hudson's Bay Company showed little interest in such a venture. James Bird, the officer in charge at Fort

Edmonton, commented that the danger and expense of expanding into the area west of the Rockies was too great to make this venture practical. For example, he described the Kutenai as a "Small" tribe and their lands "too poor to support a separate trade" in 1807. The North West Company, however, saw greater potential in the idea.

The key figure for the North West Company in this scheme was David Thompson. Thompson is generally regarded as one of the greatest explorers and cartographers in Canadian history, but he was also an important fur trader in his own right. He joined the Hudson's Bay Company as an apprentice in 1784 and had an opportunity to work with a number of the leading figures in HBC, including Samuel Hearne. His skills as a surveyor

Metis bison hunter diorama, Manitoba Museum.

and mapmaker were encouraged by HBC, and in 1792 he helped map a route from Hudson Bay to Lake Athabasca as part of HBC's campaign to compete more effectively with the NWC in that vital region. He was clearly frustrated, however, by the HBC's limited interest in surveying and exploration, and in 1797 he joined the NWC.

Thompson was initially hired by the North West Company to map the exact locations of the firm's posts. This survey had to be done because Jay's Treaty, signed in 1794, finally forced Britain, and thus Montreal fur traders as well, to abandon their posts south of the Great Lakes. American fur trade interests, particularly John Jacob Astor's American Fur Company, quickly replaced any remaining Montreal-based fur interests in the old South West trade. The treaty also indicated that a joint survey would be undertaken to establish a clear boundary in the area west of Lake Superior, and particularly Lake of the Woods. This survey work would lead to the realization that Grande Portage was actually in

American territory, as were many other significant fur trade areas, such as the upper Red River and the Missouri.

Most of this work was completed by about 1800. Thompson was increasingly involved in fur trade operations as he rose swiftly through the ranks of the North West Company to become a partner in 1804. In 1807 Thompson travelled from Rocky Mountain House, along the North Saskatchewan River, and through the front ranges of the Rockies via what is now known as Howse Pass. He then built Kootenay House near what is now Invermere, British Columbia. Soon after the post was built, a party of Peigan arrived to make their opposition known.

The Peigan "siege" of Kootenay House, which consisted primarily of camping directly outside the gate of the post, was abandoned after a few weeks, though Thompson was probably lucky that the Peigan were led by an old friend named Kootenae Appee. Had Kootenae Appee chosen to escalate the conflict into open warfare, it is not clear if Thompson and his men would have survived. The establishment of Kootenay House opened the Columbia River system to trade with the North West Company, but the hostility of the Peigan limited its initial success. As a result, the NWC was willing to consider alternatives.

By the 1770s, British, Russian, and Spanish naval expeditions had all visited the Pacific coast of North America, and the tentative beginnings of a maritime fur trade, based largely on sea otter pelts, had been established. In 1789, the Spanish built a fortified trade base at Nootka Sound, and in 1790 an agreement, the Nootka Sound Convention, was reached to allow joint trade north of San Francisco between British and Spanish interests. Not long afterwards the Spanish trade declined, but British and American traders used ships to visit key trade locations such as Nootka Sound and the Queen Charlotte Islands on a regular basis from the 1790s onwards. It was also realized that in the right circumstances, large rivers such as the Columbia could be used to establish coastal depots to serve networks of inland posts.

Iroquois cradleboard.

Like the North West Company, and to a lesser extent the Hudson's Bay Company, John Jacob Astor was also interested in establishing something like Alexander Mackenzie's transcontinental fur trade system. His vision incorporated a chain of posts extending westwards along the Missouri to the mountains, but also posts built inland from the Pacific along rivers such as the Columbia. In 1810 Astor and the NWC had opened discussions about creating a new joint venture to be called the Pacific Fur Company. The NWC was offered a one-third interest in the new venture. Thompson and other leading Nor'Westers inland knew that these discussions were underway, but they did not know that the talks had collapsed by the time Thompson began his fateful journey to the mouth of the Columbia in late 1810.

Thompson set out to reach the Columbia River system using his previous route over Howse Pass, but this time his party ran into a large and very hostile group of Peigan before reaching the mountains. The Peigan made it quite clear that Thompson and his men would not be allowed to proceed any further. Thompson was prevented from using Howse Pass, but the Peigan had little influence further north in the Athabasca River area. Thompson returned to Rocky Mountain House and redirected his path north to avoid the Peigan. He did so apparently on the advice of his Iroquois guide, Thomas.

In the late 1780s and 1790s, large numbers of eastern Canadian Indians — many of them Iroquois from Quebec — had moved west as employees of fur trade companies or to trap furs. Many married Cree or other local Aboriginal women and settled as a distinct population throughout the northwest. Fur traders often referred to these mixed bands of people as "freemen" because they were not directly associated with local First Nations, and many of the men had retired, or gone free, from fur trade company service. Across western Canada these freemen represent a major thread in the development of a distinct Métis community.

In the early 1800s, the freemen were particularly active in the area of the foothills and eastern slopes of the Rockies, and they were well established on the upper Athabasca River and the Peace and Smoky Rivers.

Fur trade records suggest that freemen bands hunted in the mountains and made use of mountain passes to reach what is now the interior plateau of British Columbia. The name Yellowhead Pass actually commemorates one such freeman, Pierre Bastonnais, or Bostonais. Bostonais was probably of mixed Iroquois and European descent, and his surname suggests he may have come originally from the United States. He was usually known, however, by his nickname "Tête Jaune," or "Yellowhead," bestowed because of his fair hair.

Thomas, Thompson's mountain guide, also seems to have been aware of the use of mountain passes by his fellow Iroquois freemen and understood that the Athabasca River

Plains Cree dress made of deerskin.

was well to the north of any possible Peigan threat. In December 1810, Thompson and his party reached the Jasper area and began preparations for a mid-winter crossing of Athabasca Pass. Thompson's account of this grim journey makes compelling reading, but the significance of the journey does not lie in its hardships. From the western end of Athabasca Pass, Thompson was able to reach the Columbia River system, which meant Howse Pass was no longer vital.

Thompson proceeded down the Columbia, mapping it with great precision and travelling with no apparent sense of urgency. As a result, he arrived at its mouth in mid-July 1811 only to discover employees of Astor's Pacific Fur Company busy constructing a post, Fort Astoria, there. While Thompson was travelling overland from Athabasca Pass, Astor's party had sailed around Cape Horn and then north along the Pacific coast of the Americas. By beating Thompson, Americans would later claim a right to trade in the region.

Historians have long debated the significance of Thompson's 1810–11 actions. No one questions his skill as a mapmaker or explorer. However, some have suggested he showed little of the audacious "North West" spirit, first in avoiding a confrontation with the Peigan and then in not making a mad dash for the mouth of the Columbia. Other historians have noted that offering a direct challenge to the Peigan would have been foolhardy and unproductive. It might have cost the North West Company the trade of a large and powerful First Nation and risked the larger plan of encouraging trade with the Columbia River peoples. As for racing to beat the Americans to the mouth of the Columbia, Thompson had no reason to believe such urgency was necessary. Thompson and other the NWC officers in the field had no way of knowing that Astor and the Pacific Fur Company had become rivals rather than partners in the Columbia venture.

The presence of the Pacific Fur Company at Fort Astoria had little immediate impact on the North West Company, which continued to dominate the fur trade throughout most of the Columbia River system. The Pacific Fur Company did build some

inland posts, including Fort Okanagan near the mouth of the Okanagan River, but the War of 1812 dealt the company a serious blow. In 1813 Astor had difficulty arranging shipping to supply Fort Astoria, while the NWC was able to outfit a ship, the *Isaac Todd*, to sail with a Royal Navy escort for the Columbia River.

Under the circumstances, the partners of the Pacific Fur Company felt compelled to admit defeat and follow the lead of the old XY Company. The partners in the Pacific Fur Company sold their interest in Fort Astoria, Fort Okanagan, and other posts for 10 per cent above their initial investment and temporarily abandoned the fur trade of the Pacific northwest.

By 1813 the North West Company had succeeded in creating a genuinely transcontinental trade system along the lines envisioned by Alexander Mackenzie years earlier. However, in retrospect it is easy to see that the NWC's successes hid serious problems. Supplying posts in New Caledonia and on the Columbia and Mackenzie Rivers was expensive and time consuming, and elsewhere in the North West the company faced more effective and aggressive competition from a revitalized Hudson's Bay Company.

Despite its efforts to expand north and westwards towards the Arctic and Pacific Oceans, the key area for the North West Company's profits remained the Athabasca region. In recognition of this reality, in 1799 the Hudson's Bay Company sent one its best traders, Peter Fidler, to build posts on the fringes of the Athabasca area at Ile à la Crosse and Meadow Lake in what is now northern Saskatchewan. Fidler then built Greenwich House near Lac La Biche on the height of land between the Arctic and Hudson Bay drainage systems. Finally, in 1802 Fidler built Nottingham House on Lake Athabasca to compete directly with the NWC's neighbouring Fort Chipewyan.

The XY Company was also active in the area at the time, and Fidler's journals reveal the effect this competition had on company costs. When Pond first arrived in the area, he traded so many furs he could not bring them all out in the first year. As late as 1799, the North West Company took 15

North West Company's beaver token from 1820.

The Governor of the Red River, Hudson's Bay, Voyaging in a Light Canoe, by Peter Rindisbacher.

partially loaded canoes of trade goods into the Athabasca district and in return secured 648 packs, or 30 tonnes, of "excellent furs." By comparison, Fidler calculated that in 1803, the NWC secured about 1 pack of furs for every 4 packs of trade goods it brought into the Athabasca district, and that the Hudson's Bay Company and XY Company were, if anything, even less successful. He calculated his total returns at Nottingham House in 1803 as a scant 6 bundles of furs worth a little more than 253 made beaver. Still, HBC persevered and prevented the NWC from trading completely unopposed in the area.

Not only did the increased competition cut profit margins on trade, but it also led to rising levels of violence as the Nor'Westers tried to use their larger numbers to harass and intimidate their rivals' employees. Perhaps even more ruinously, the violence spread into relations with Aboriginal groups. This type of conflict was not new — the Iroquois Wars and Pontiac's War indicated that violence was always a potential aspect of cross-cultural trade and contact — but it was relatively rare. In the early 1800s, however, the fur trade became more cutthroat, and in the Athabasca area in particular, numbers of Aboriginal peoples

Thomas Douglas, fifth Earl of Selkirk and founder of the Red River Settlement.

simply withdrew from the trade.

The Nor'Westers bought out the XY Company, but this was only a partial solution to the problem. In 1803, the North West Company sent a ship to Hudson Bay to explore the idea of supplying its posts using essentially the same routes and techniques as the Hudson's Bay Company. Nothing came of the venture, but in 1804 the NWC initiated a meeting with HBC to discuss the idea of working in concert to manage the fur trade and perhaps use HBC posts on Hudson Bay and James Bay to supply both companies' inland posts.

The time was not yet right for such a coalition of interests, and the Hudson's Bay Company responded by noting that such a plan would undermine its charter rights and very business. Still, the North West Company persevered and actually offered HBC £2,000 a year for the right to ship trade goods and furs via York Factory. When HBC turned this offer down, another approach was planned.

Because the fur trade was in such financial disarray, the value of shares in the Hudson's Bay Company had dropped sharply. Shares once worth £250 were selling for between £50 and £60, and in 1808 plans were made for the North West Company to purchase a controlling interest in HBC. The specific details of the story remain a mystery, but apparently Alexander Mackenzie, with support from William and Simon McGillivray, two leading figures in the NWC, began to buy HBC shares as they came on the market. This purchasing had to be done in a clandestine fashion, since transfers of shares had to be reported to the governor and committee of HBC. If it became obvious that Nor'Westers were buying shares the plan could be stopped, so Mackenzie and the McGillivrays had to use an intermediary.

Their choice for this role was a Scottish aristocrat, Thomas Douglas, the Earl of Selkirk. Selkirk was a quite remarkable man with broad political, social, and business interests. He took a particular interest in the problem of Scottish and Irish emigration. Large numbers of Scottish and Irish families had been thrown out of work and into dire poverty by changes in agriculture in the late 18th and early 19th centuries. As landowners tried to maximize their returns, they often ousted small tenants in order to enclose land and use it to raise sheep or other profitable crops. Both Scotland and Ireland had growing populations of poor, displaced agricultural labourers, and Selkirk believed that assisting these families to immigrate to British North America would strengthen both Britain and the colonies.

As early as 1802, Selkirk had speculated that the area around Lake Winnipeg and Red River might be a suitable location for a colony of Scottish and Irish emigrants,

The Winnipeg River was one of the major transportation routes to the interior used by Montreal-based fur trade companies.

Aerial photograph of the reconstructed Fort William at Thunder Bay, Ontario.

although his first actual attempts to resettle Scots in British North America were in Prince Edward Island and at Baldoon in Upper Canada. Nonetheless, it is easy to see how Mackenzie and Selkirk might make common cause. Mackenzie was interested in reorganizing the fur trade by gaining control of the Hudson's Bay Company, while Selkirk could establish a colony and profit at the same time as his shares in HBC increased in value.

The actual extent of this cooperation is not known, but records suggest that Mackenzie and Selkirk had some sort of agreement to work together, purchasing Hudson's Bay Company shares with an eye to transferring them later to Mackenzie and William McGillivray. At some point, however, Selkirk changed his mind.

Selkirk's brother-in-law, Andrew Wedderburn, or Wedderburn-Colvile, played a key role in this convoluted story. In 1810, Wedderburn-Colvile drew up a plan to reorganize the Hudson's Bay Company to make it more profitable. The plan involved dividing the company's operations into two large regions, each headed by a superintendent. Within these regions, large areas he called "factories" were set up, paralleling the North West Company's idea of districts. The real changes embodied in the plan, however, were that HBC officers would no longer be paid just a salary; they would be paid a smaller base salary supplemented by a share of the profits from the trade of their respective factories. The intent was to give company officers a direct financial interest in the success of their districts. This scheme was borrowed directly from the NWC, which paid its "wintering partners" on this same profit-sharing principle.

In addition, Wedderburn-Colvile proposed that the Hudson's Bay Company reduce its reliance on hiring employees in the Orkneys, as it was felt Orkneymen were too easily intimidated by aggressive Nor'Westers. Instead, HBC would try to hire more Scots from the Highlands and Western Islands on the grounds that they were a "more spirited race" than Orcadians. Finally, Wedderburn-Colvile proposed a program of cutting costs, primarily through reducing imports of food and other supplies by making more productive use of post employees and their families.

The latter proposal was not completely new but rather an extension of ideas already current within the management of the Hudson's Bay Company. HBC had finally officially recognized the existence of families at its posts in the 1790s and made some effort to recruit new employees from among the children living at posts. In 1802 the annual letter from York Factory to the London Committee described the women at the post as "virtually" servants — or employees — of the company and listed their services:

> …they clean and put into a state of preservation all
> Beavr. and Otter skins…. They prepare Line for
> Snow shoes and knit them also without which your
> Honors servants could not give efficient opposition
> to the Canadian traders they make Leather shoes
> …and are usefull in a variety of other instances…

In 1806 HBC even proposed establishing schools at its main posts to educate the children living there, although this suggestion was not entirely altruistic. The intent was make such posts "…a Colony of very useful Hands."

In addition to recognizing the work of the families of company employees and using that labour to reduce costs, Wedderburn-Colvile's plan also meshed with Selkirk's hopes. On May 29, 1811, less than a year after the reorganization scheme had been adopted by the Hudson's Bay Company, Selkirk was offered a grant of land to be called Assiniboia. This land grant consisted of over 300,000 square kilometres

of land around the Red River and Assiniboine River. Selkirk faced minimal obligations in return. The most significant of these were that he was expected to settle 1,000 families on the land within 10 years, that he would provide 200 new employees a year for HBC, and grant land to retiring HBC employees within the settlement. The hope was that the colony would assist HBC by providing a ready pool of new employees and a reliable source of agricultural products to lower the costs of importing food.

This proposal was passed by a shareholders meeting, but not without controversy. Alexander Mackenzie voted against it, and other the North West Company supporters were barred from voting their shares on the grounds that they had held them for less than six months. Several other large shareholders voted against the proposal, but it did pass comfortably in the end. Selkirk and Wedderburn-Colvile obviously supported it, but they controlled about only 20 per cent of the company's shares at this time and could scarcely force their views on the company. Nevertheless, the NWC and Alexander Mackenzie were incensed at what they saw as Selkirk's deception and the threat the proposed colony posed to the Nor'Westers.

Personal animosity aside, it is easy to see why the North West Company was so opposed to this idea. Selkirk's land grant sat directly astride the main canoe route from Fort William to Lake Winnipeg. Equally importantly, it also was located in the midst of one of the best buffalo hunting areas in the North West, the Red and Assiniboine River valleys. A large population of settlers could threaten the NWC supplies of pemmican just at a time when the company was most in need of these supplies to help maintain its strained transportation system. In addition, this area was not uninhabited. There were Cree and Saulteaux living nearby, but the Red River area was also home to a growing population of Métis with close family and economic ties to the NWC. The actions of the London Committee may have been well meaning, but granting a huge tract of land to Selkirk for a pittance, based on an equally questionable original company charter, was a cavalier act.

Selkirk began to recruit labourers in Scotland and Ireland both for the Hudson's Bay Company and to help establish his colony. He also selected Miles Macdonell to act as the first governor of the settlement. Macdonell was an interesting choice for the task. He was related to several the North West Company officers and knew many more, as he had lived in the old Loyalist settlements near Cornwall in Upper Canada. Rather than reducing animosity, choosing Macdonell seems to have increased it further, since he too seemed a turncoat to the Nor'Westers.

For their part, Nor'Westers and their supporters in Scotland set about trying to undermine Selkirk's efforts to recruit his quota of labourers. This resistance included publishing a letter in the *Inverness Journal* that suggested potential recruits faced hugely exaggerated perils such as "2000 Miles of Inland Navigation — stemming strong currents and dangerous rapids & carrying boats and cargoes over numerous portages." On arrival they would find themselves surrounded by hostile "natives" so that:

> Even if [they] escape the scalping knife, they will be subject to constant alarm and terror. Their habitations, their Crops, their Cattle will be destroyed and they will find it impossible to exist in the Country.

The result was that the process of finding recruits dragged on until late in the summer, and many deserted right up until the Hudson's Bay Company's ships finally left port in Stornoway. Selkirk and Macdonell secured a fraction of the men they had hoped to recruit, and the departure was so delayed there was no chance that they could get inland to Red River that same year. Instead they had to stay at York Factory in a hastily constructed and quite inadequate camp for the winter. Scurvy soon followed, and by mid-winter, tempers frayed. Fights broke out among the men, and from February to May there was an open mutiny against Macdonell.

In the end, the mutiny was quashed, but it was not until early July that Macdonell and a small party of men left for Red River. They reached the proposed site of Selkirk's colony on September 1, 1812 — far too late in the year to plant crops or make much progress building houses for the winter. When a second party arrived from York Factory in late October, Macdonell sent most to winter upriver at Pembina. There at least they had some prospect of food from the buffalo herds nearby. Somewhat surprisingly, the North West

Company officials in Red River were helpful at first. Colonists and fur traders generally left each other alone, and the tiny colony staggered along with small numbers of new settlers, including families, arriving every year.

Still, food was always a problem, and in January 1814, Miles Macdonell, as governor of Assiniboia, tried to ensure that any available food would be used in the settlement first. He issued the notorious Pemmican Proclamation, which stated that no pemmican could be exported from Assiniboia for a year. This proclamation had little impact on the Hudson's Bay Company, which used far less pemmican than the Nor'Westers. Instead, it was a real threat to the Nor'Westers, who needed large supplies of pemmican from the Red and Assiniboine River areas for the canoe brigades. Later that year Macdonell also issued a proclamation banning "running" buffalo with horses. This regulation annoyed the Métis buffalo hunters living in the area, especially as they felt Macdonell had no legal jurisdiction over their actions.

Both proclamations seemed to suggest that Macdonell and Selkirk were trying to use the colony to undermine the interests of the North West Company and the Red River Métis. Relations between the colonists and the Métis and the NWC deteriorated rapidly. The Nor'Westers spent the winter of 1814–15 convincing most of the settlers to abandon Red River. If they did so, they were promised passage out to Upper Canada and new land there. By the spring of 1815, most were ready to take up this offer.

The methods of persuasion were not subtle. Some colonists were ready to leave voluntarily, but others were convinced by a combination of threats and open harassment. Macdonell was arrested by the Nor'Westers and sent to Upper Canada. The settlement was temporarily abandoned until Macdonell's successor, Robert Semple, and new party of colonists arrived later that summer.

Ill feelings escalated over the winter, and in the spring of 1816, Hudson's Bay Company employees seized the North West Company post in Red River, Fort Gibraltar. The NWC countered, and Cuthbert Grant, an NWC officer and leader of the Red River Métis, seized Brandon House and its stock of pemmican. Grant then sent the pemmican with an armed guard to meet the NWC's brigades at Red River.

This was not normal practice and clearly suggests that the

Métis anticipated some sort of incident when they arrived at Red River. Earlier in March, Grant had threatened a "warm reception" for colonists and the Hudson's Bay Company from the Métis, and he hoped to "never see any of them again in the Colonizing way in Red River." Despite this war of escalating words and threatened violence, however, most suspect that ensuing events were unplanned and went far beyond anything anticipated by Grant or the North West Company.

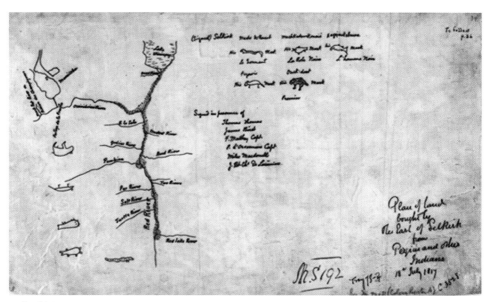

Selkirk Treaty Map, circa 1817.

When Grant and his supporters reached Red River on June 19, 1816, Robert Semple and an armed group of settlers intercepted them at a place called Seven Oaks. What happened next is shrouded in mystery, but when Semple confronted the Métis, a shot was fired. As historian Jack Bumstead has noted:

> In the ensuing battle the [Métis] had all the advantages. Most of the settlers were not soldiers and were unfamiliar with guns, while their opponents — hunters and plainsmen — used them almost daily.

As a result, the battle was short and utterly decisive. Twenty-one settlers, including Semple, were killed, along with just one member of Grant's party.

For decades historians debated who was to blame for Seven Oaks: Grant, the Métis, the North West Company, Semple, Macdonell, Selkirk, the Hudson's Bay Company, even the dead colonists themselves who lacked the wit to realize that confronting the Métis was a foolish and provocative act. Increasingly, however, most feel that assigning blame for a situation that everyone played a part in creating is not terribly enlightening. The battle itself and the loss of 22 lives were almost certainly not premeditated, but they were a completely logical consequence of five years of escalating tension and misunderstanding between Selkirk's settlers and the Red River Métis and the NWC.

In the aftermath of the battle, Grant demanded that the Hudson's Bay Company's fort at Red River, Fort Douglas, be handed over, and once again the settlement was dispersed. Senior North West Company officials commended Grant and his chief supporters for their actions, and Pierre Falcon, a Métis musician, composed a song celebrating the great victory at Seven Oaks. In time many other people, including the freemen of the Athabasca River and foothills areas, and the

Seven Oaks House, Winnipeg.

Factor's House, Fort Dunvegan.

families of fur trade company employees throughout the north, would also come to be known as Métis. However, most historians believe the dispute with the Selkirk settlers and the Battle at Seven Oaks were really key events in creating the idea that the Métis were a distinct people or nation with a special connection to the Red River area.

The North West Company seemed in complete control of the situation in Red River, but this quickly proved an illusion. Selkirk had previously arrived in Lower Canada in September 1815 to marshal support for his colony at Red River. He lobbied political, military, and business leaders and tried to keep abreast of events in the North West. He also set about recruiting a private army to help defend his settlement. To this end, he convinced about 90 members of the disbanded De Meuron regiment, which had fought in the War of 1812, to accompany him to Red River in the summer of 1816.

Selkirk received word of the violent confrontation at Seven Oaks before he left for Red River with his retired soldiers. Clearly incensed and seeking some sort of legal or financial recompense, Selkirk reached Fort William on Lake Superior in August. In a move of singular boldness — but dubious legality — Selkirk captured Fort William and arrested any Nor'Westers he found there who might have been implicated in the Red River troubles. He then shipped the prisoners back to Upper Canada for trial. From Fort William, Selkirk sent his De Meuron forces inland to capture posts and prepare to retake Red River. In late December they finally reached Red River, recapturing Fort Daer at Pembina

and Fort Douglas at Red River.

In just over six months, Selkirk had reversed the situation in Red River completely, but his aggressive response produced a political reaction. The Nor'Westers were still well connected in political circles in both the Canadas and Britain, and there was considerable sympathy for their cause. The Colonial Office in London suggested that events were no longer just a commercial dispute, but something that the courts needed to resolve. In Canada, a special commission of inquiry headed by William Coltman was created and sent west in 1817. When the commission reached Red River, it busied itself with collecting depositions from participants in the battle of Seven Oaks — who all happened to be Métis or North West Company employees, since Semple and his supporters could scarcely testify. Coltman also interviewed Selkirk, along with settlers and local Cree and Saulteaux, but Selkirk and his supporters were convinced that Coltman and the entire commission were quite unsympathetic to their position. In addition, while everyone awaited Coltman's report, Selkirk and the Nor'Westers initiated a series of civil and criminal legal actions against each other that slowly dragged through the courts over the next years.

Coltman's final report, delivered in 1818, was far more objective and impartial than Selkirk had feared it might be, but impartiality probably favoured the North West Company. Coltman suggested that assigning blame for the violence that had occurred in Red River and the Athabasca area was probably beyond even the power of the courts to ascertain. Instead he proposed either the return of property to all parties or the payment of compensation for property was lost or destroyed. His hope was to restore stability, and in effect he argued for a return to something like the pre-1816 status quo.

The situation prior to 1816 actually suited the Nor'Westers, but it left Selkirk still aggrieved and the victims of Seven Oaks still victims. It is hard to say how events might have been resolved had Selkirk not died early in 1820. Arguably, his death removed a major impediment to a resolution of what Jack Bumstead has termed the "Fur Trade Wars."

Equally important in these wars were the rising costs and declining profits of fur trade companies. It has been estimated that by 1820, the Hudson's Bay Company was over £100,000 in debt. This figure is roughly double the total value of company shares that were represented at the shareholders meeting that granted Selkirk his land in 1811. Legal proceedings and other costs had also bitten heavily into the finances of the North West Company, and this had a very serious operational consequence. The wintering partners of the NWC were paid from trade profits, and these profits were falling sharply. Discontent with the situation was obvious by 1819, and by 1820 the wintering partners, who managed posts and traded for furs, were ready to initiate a truly dramatic change.

A group of wintering partners approached the Hudson's Bay Company informally to see if HBC would consider supplying them with trade goods and handling sales of the furs they acquired. Had this happened, the Montreal and London agents of the North West Company would have been left with few, if any, traders in the field once the current agreement with the wintering partners ended in 1822. The NWC would effectively cease to exist.

Andrew Wedderburn-Colvile was unsure how the Hudson's Bay Company could act as supplier and agent for the very traders with whom it was competing for furs but thought some other arrangement might be possible. He preferred some sort of merger or coalition of the two companies'

operations. In 1810 Wedderburn-Colvile had based his reorganization of HBC's operations on trying to reduce costs and improve efficiency, and he believed that a merged fur trade company could achieve even greater economies.

Wedderburn-Colvile offered the North West Company an alternative proposal: a grand coalition of business interests. If the two firms merged, profits could be distributed on a preassigned basis to the old wintering partners, existing senior Hudson's Bay Company officers, the agents of the NWC, existing HBC shareholders, and the Selkirk estate in compensation for his losses in Red River. Things were desperate enough that, although some negotiation was still required, the proposal met with general agreement. On March 26, 1821, all parties signed.

The Colonial Office, which had viewed the events of 1816 with great concern, was very pleased with this turn of events. In fact, there was almost certainly subtle political pressure on all parties to end the ruinous disputes sooner by negotiation rather than later in the courts. In response to the merger, the Colonial Office gave the new company, which retained the Hudson's Bay Company name, a valuable extension of its trading privileges. This extension was to run for 21 years and included not just the area covered by the old HBC Charter, but the areas incorporated into the North West Company's operations following Mackenzie's voyages. Thus the new company secured exclusive trade rights in the Athabasca, Mackenzie, New Caledonia, and Columbia districts as well.

It seemed a happy conclusion all around, at least for the owners and senior officers of the new company. Implementing the coalition of the companies in the field — as opposed to the stock exchange — would prove a more wrenching task for employees and their families.

Andrew's Church was the centre of the agricultural settlement that grew up south of Lower Fort Garry on the Red River.

7

Fur Trade Monopoly — The George Simpson Era, 1821–1849

Historians still debate the implications of the merger of the Hudson's Bay and the North West companies. Did the NWC finally succeed in capturing the HBC from within? Did the merger mark the triumph of the conservative HBC over the more entrepreneurial and aggressive Nor'Westers? Former Nor'Westers, including many who got their start in the fur trade with the old XY Company, held a disproportionate number of senior officer positions in the reorganized the HBC. However, the overall direction of the fur trade — management of the company as a whole, exemplified by the choice of London to serve as the firm's head office — tended to fall into the hands of former HBC officials. In part, this was a product of the remarkable influence of George Simpson on the management of the new firm.

Simpson began his career in the fur trade in 1820, just as the Hudson's Bay and the North West companies were beginning the final stages of their long competition and the initial stages of their amalgamation. Simpson was sent to Fort Wedderburn on Lake Athabasca to organize the HBC's operations in the vital Athabasca district as part of his grooming for future advancement within the HBC. Historian E. E. Rich has suggested somewhat optimistically that while at Fort Wedderburn, Simpson "ran across almost every aspect of the fur trade…and by the time he came out to Norway House in

May and June 1821 he was already as complete a master of the problems of the Canadian fur trade as anyone had ever been."

It was on this trip back to Norway House that Simpson learned the two companies had been amalgamated and that he had been appointed as one of two overseas governors to take charge of the operations of the new company. The fur trade was to be divided into two departments: The Southern Department was responsible for trade based in the area from James Bay south to the Great Lakes and east into what is now northern Quebec and Labrador. Simpson initially was given control over the Northern Department, the larger of the two and the more critical to the new company's business success, as it stretched from what is now northwestern Ontario west to the Pacific and north to the edges of the Arctic Ocean.

In many respects, it was a bold and unusual move to put Simpson in charge. He had just one winter's experience in the fur trade and was faced with the challenges of integrating the operations of two very different companies and their often mutually hostile workforces. Simpson was, however, an experienced businessman, having worked for over a decade in a London sugar brokerage. He was also a remarkably quick study, and he had the invaluable business trait of complete assurance that his opinions and decisions were

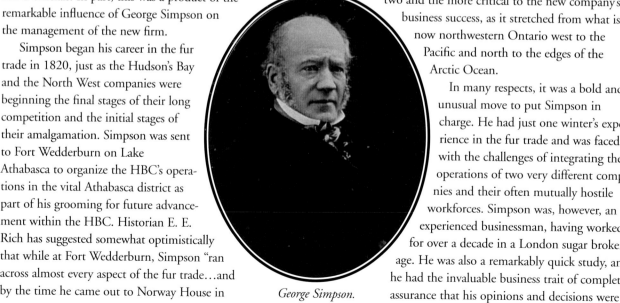

George Simpson.

correct. Simpson did make some questionable business decisions in his first years as governor of the Northern Department, particularly in the areas of transportation routes and attempts to diversify the economy of the settlement at Red River. Still, his employers obviously believed his character and experience were ideal for the job. Moreover, he did have the advantage that he had not really played any significant role in any of the "fur trade wars" prior to the merger. As a result, he was an acceptable leader to both former Nor'Westers and the Hudson's Bay Company officers.

George Simpson dominated the fur trade throughout most of what is now Canada and parts of the United States from 1821 until his death at Lachine in 1860. Simpson's influence literally became continent-wide after 1826, when he was placed in charge of the Hudson's Bay Company's entire operation in North America.

Simpson's first task in 1821, however, was to reorganize the fur trade in the Northern Department in order to make it efficient and profitable again. To do this, he and the new the Hudson's Bay Company concentrated their efforts in three main areas: integrating the operations and personnel of the two former companies, reorganizing trade and transportation systems, and continuing to reduce costs by making the fur trade more self-sufficient. Many of the ideas that were implemented can really be traced back to Alexander Mackenzie, Andrew Wedderburn-Colvile, and other earlier figures, but it was George Simpson who managed to put them into effect.

The first and most obvious item of business was integrating two largely parallel company organizations. The old Hudson's Bay Company had little presence in New Caledonia, on the Columbia, or on the Gulf of St. Lawrence.

The North West Company, for its part, had had little interest in the areas around Hudson Bay. In these areas there was little need for major change and the new company simply took over existing posts and continued to operate them. However, across a broad area from what is now northern Quebec to the Rockies, the two companies had operated parallel systems of posts and had often built posts in marginal trade areas to forestall their opponents.

The "Depot Warehouse" at York Factory. After 1713, York Factory emerged as the largest of the HBC's bayside posts. This 19th century building reflects York Factory's role as the administrative and transshipment centre for the company.

As a result, the new Hudson's Bay Company was able to reduce the number of posts it operated sharply. By 1830 only 41 posts were needed for the entire Northern Department, although this figure was increased by fluctuating numbers of temporary seasonal outposts, most staffed by just an employee or two. For example, Fort Augustus and Fort Edmonton were amalgamated into a single post, as were Acton House and Rocky Mountain House, and Fort Wedderburn and Fort Chipewyan. Many smaller and less profitable posts were simply closed and never replaced. Even with these post closures and amalgamations, however, the new HBC maintained posts in virtually every area of what is now Canada, from Labrador and the Gulf of St. Lawrence to the Pacific Ocean and north to the Arctic.

Fort Edmonton.

ture that combined elements of both companies' former systems. A portion of company profits, set at 40 percent, was used to pay a new group of senior employees called "commissioned" officers. This fund was initially divided into 85 shares. These men were roughly the equivalent of the old wintering partners, but they were quite clearly employees — albeit well-paid ones. The new company established two grades of commissioned officers: chief factors who received two shares of the profit pool each, and chief traders who received a single share. Chief factors were usually placed in charge of an entire fur trade district, such as New Caledonia, Red River, or the Saskatchewan. The work of chief traders was more varied. Many commanded major posts, such as Fort Edmonton or York Factory, while others took charge of specific business functions, such as coordinating the transportation system or looking after the trade accounts.

Commissioned officers were well paid. Although their income could vary from year to year based on trade returns, it is estimated that between 1821 and 1872, a single share in the commissioned officers' fund was worth £360 a year on average. By comparison, a company labourer earned about £17 to £20 a year, meaning that many posts were marked by stark differences in wealth and privilege. Given the limited number of commissions available, competition for them was fierce, and many senior North West Company and the Hudson's Bay Company officials left the trade in 1821 when it became clear that they had no place in the new regime.

Commissioned officers were to be selected from the ranks of senior salaried officers, who were paid a contracted salary for their services and were assigned different titles, or "ranks," in what resembled a military social structure. Most were designated as "clerks" and paid a gradually increasing rate up to a maximum of about £100 a year. Other officers were designated as "postmasters." They generally looked after smaller, less crucial posts or served as

Daniel Williams Harmon, fur trader.

The result was also a massive reduction in employment and an excellent early example of "right-sizing," as modern business consultants like to call it. Together, the North West Company and the Hudson's Bay Company had employed some 1,927 men in British North America as full-time employees in 1821. By 1826 this figure was reduced to just 694 men, or just over a third of the original number. Thereafter, the size of the company's workforce began to grow again until it stabilized at about 1,000 men in the 1830s. These job cuts affected employees at every level in the company, from senior officers to labourers, and in most cases the cuts also affected the families of company employees.

The new company adopted a hybrid employment struc-

Upper Fort Garry gate, Winnipeg.

junior officers in large posts such as Fort Edmonton or York Factory. The final category of officers were apprentice clerks and postmasters — young men starting their careers who might be paid just £20 per annum. This figure might have been less than what many tradesmen made, but the new Hudson's Bay Company drew a sharp distinction between officers and the men. Whatever their pay, even the most junior of apprentice postmasters were accorded the status of gentleman. This meant they ate in the officers' mess, they lived in the officers' quarters, and, when travelling by canoe or York boat, they did not have to paddle or row and had separate fires and tents when camping. In fact, fur trade communities, even tiny posts with just a handful of employees, were structured in a careful hierarchy that governed everything from what they wore and ate to how they travelled and what they did for entertainment.

The men were also organized hierarchically. The new Hudson's Bay Company paid tradesmen, such as blacksmiths, armourers, boatbuilders, coopers, and tinsmiths, between £25 and £50 a year based on their experience and skills. The numbers of tradesmen employed by the company underlines both the complexity of maintaining posts and equipment — hence the need for carpenters, joiners, and boatbuilders — and a growing desire to manufacture locally as many trade goods as possible as a way of reducing costs. York Factory and Upper

Fort Garry in particular became significant producers of trade items such as tinware and iron goods in the years after 1821. Other employees were paid for their mastery of more specifically fur trade skills. Skilled canoe- and boatmen, particularly the men designated as guides, steersmen, and bowsmen, were paid up to £30 or £35 a year. Interpreters, who spoke Aboriginal languages, were held in even higher regard and might earn up to £40 a year for their labour. Men designated as labourers or ordinary boat- and canoemen, who were called midmen, or *milieux*, after their place in boats and canoes, made up the largest single category of employees. They tended to be paid between £17 and £20 a year.

In all cases, the Hudson's Bay Company also provided food, housing, and some clothing and other items to its employees, and most of the married men also received some support for their wives and children living at posts. This meant that fur trade incomes were actually much higher than they appeared, and comparative figures suggest that the HBC employees were paid as well or better than people doing equivalent work in Britain or the Canadas. For example, a chief trader's income of about £360 a year in the 1830s would be roughly equivalent in purchasing power to CDN $48,000 in 2004. Given that a chief trader paid no tax on this income and his basic living expenses were covered, an equivalent modern salary might be closer to $100,000 a

Cart from Upper Fort Garry, Winnipeg.

year or more. By comparison, a labourer's salary would translate to between $2,000 and $3,000 a year in disposable income, making them better off than most labourers in Britain in the early 19th century, who rarely earned much above their essential living costs.

The new company also had an opportunity to reorganize the logistics of its trade and transportation system, continuing a long process that can be dated back to the 1790s and Wedderburn-Colvile's attempts in 1810–11 to restructure the old Hudson's Bay Company.

When the Hudson's Bay Company first began operating posts inland from Hudson and James bays in the 1770s, it had to rely on purchasing canoes from Aboriginal groups. These canoes had a limited cargo capacity, and the HBC struggled both to supply its inland posts and to find employees with sufficient skill to take canoes inland. In the 1790s,

the HBC began to experiment with using a new type of watercraft. The "invention" of the York boat is sometimes credited to George Sutherland, a trader at Fort Edmonton in 1795, but it really is based on traditional Orkney boat designs. In fact, roughly similar boats had been used on the Albany River by the company as early as the late 1740s and 1750s, and in the Canadas, *bateaux,* or open wooden cargo boats, were also in common use.

York boats were built in various sizes, with keels ranging from about 9 to 14 metres, or 28 to 45 feet. The smaller boats tended to be used on the Saskatchewan River, while the larger boats were used between York Factory and Norway House at the north end of Lake Winnipeg. Depending upon their size, these boats could transport a cargo of between 2,500 and 5,000 kilograms. The smaller York boats had double the capacity of the North West Company's *canot du nord*

York boat re-enactment.

Southwest bastion, Lower Fort Garry.

and surpassed the capacity even of the large *canot du maître* used between Fort William and Montreal. York boats required roughly the same crew of eight to ten men, however, as a *canot du nord*. A crew consisted of a bowsman and steersman, and six to eight men to pull the long oars that powered the vessel. York boats could be sailed on large open bodies of water, poled in shallow rivers, and tracked like canoes by pulling them on lines against the current. Because wages were such a large part of the costs of production of furs, the York boat gave the old Hudson's Bay Company a significant economic advantage over its rivals, since it allowed the HBC to move more weight of cargo per employee than the Nor'Westers.

The York boat did have drawbacks, which explains why the Nor'Westers rarely used similar boats or *bateaux* in their operations. They were slower than canoes and cumbersome to portage. The Hudson's Bay Company was able to accept these problems because its transportation route inland was much shorter, and time — while important — was less critical than it was for the Nor'Westers, who had to move furs from the Mackenzie River and New Caledonia to Fort William and then trade goods back

Lower Fort Garry blacksmith.

within a single season.

Many historians believe that the use of York boats and the ability to ship goods directly from Britain to ports on Hudson Bay and James Bay gave the Hudson's Bay Company a crucial advantage over the Nor'Westers and helped force the amalgamation of the two companies. Simpson and the new owners of the HBC appear to have agreed with this assessment, because after 1821, the new company effectively abandoned the use of canoes on an old transportation route from Montreal to Fort William. The route was used on occasion by travellers, including George Simpson, who in later years chose to live in Lachine near Montreal, but after 1821 Fort William and Montreal declined as fur trade centres. Similarly, canoes were used on occasion — once again, Simpson liked to travel by canoe with a crew of handpicked voyageurs and his personal bagpiper, Colin Fraser, since this enabled him to travel at speed and arrive at posts in style — but after 1821 the York boat replaced canoes as the main bulk carrier of the fur trade.

William McGillivray commented gloomily that following the merger, "the Fur Trade is for ever lost to Canada!" Although not strictly true, since furs continued to be traded in Upper and Lower Canada and in the Maritime colonies as well, his comment is a fair assessment of the situation after 1821, and it was not until the 1860s that Canada began to take a real interest in the North West once again.

The final aspect of Simpson's reorganization of the fur trade was a continued emphasis on cutting costs and making the fur trade more self-sufficient. Reducing the number of posts and the number of company employees and their families living at posts had an immediate impact on the profitability of the new company. In 1821 the total wage bill for the Northern Department stood at £53,451. By 1830, the payroll of the Hudson's Bay Company for salaried officers and the men in the Northern Department was just less than £11,000, although the shares paid to commissioned officers would have added to this total. Costs did increase over time, but in 1857 the basic wage bill for the Northern Department remained at roughly £14,700 a year.

These reductions in wage costs were not matched by any equivalent loss of trade. In fact, in many areas the quantities of furs traded increased after 1821. In the Mackenzie River district, for example, production increased from 111 packs of furs in 1821 to 157 packs in 1827. Company accounts also indicate that the new company was generally profitable and, although specific profit levels varied from year to year, the entire period from 1821 to the 1840s, in historian A. S. Morton's words, was marked "by profound quiet, [and] by an extraordinarily successful fur trade."

Reducing the workforce paradoxically may have improved the self-sufficiency of the fur trade. The

Métis families, such as the one pictured here, made up over 80 percent of the population in Red River by 1871.

human cost of such massive reductions in employment should not be underestimated, and fur trade records are filled with accounts of just how great a wrench this change was for the men, who found themselves out of work with the new company, and for their families. Those who could afford it retired to Britain or the Canadas, sometimes with their families and sometimes not, but most had no choice but to stay on and adjust to the new situation.

Hundreds of former fur trade employees and their families moved to Red River, and it was only after 1821 that Selkirk's old colony really began to be established on a firm footing. Census figures underline the impact of this population movement. In 1821 Red River had a population of just 419 people, over half of whom were Scots. In addition, about 500 Métis lived further upriver at Pembina, the former Fort Daer, just south of what is now the border between Manitoba and North Dakota. By 1849, the population of Red River had increased five times to more than 5,200 people.

In the process, the idea that the settlement would serve as a haven for displaced Scottish settlers was lost. Instead, Red River increasingly became a Métis settlement, composed of both English-speaking Métis — the Country-born or Mixed Bloods — and the better-known French-speaking Métis. By 1871, out of a population of roughly 12,000 people, 5,000 were French-speaking Métis and 5,000 were English-speaking Mixed Bloods. Although the two groups were distinct in some respects and Red River was marked in later years by separate Protestant and Catholic, English, and French-speaking parishes and communities, there were always close ties of kinship and business interest that linked Métis and Mixed Blood people throughout the entire Red River settlement.

The other option for individuals and families who were displaced after 1821 was not to relocate at all, but to remain living and working in the same area as before. Some joined local bands if they had close kinship ties with First Nations groups. Others opted to associate themselves with the bands of freemen that had been growing in numbers and influence since the 1790s. Historian Heather Devine has studied members of the Desjarlais family very closely, and her genealogical research suggests that different members of the same family came to identify themselves as Cree and Ojibwa, Métis, and Canadien. After 1821, in many parts of the North West, identity became less a matter of ancestry than way of life. Put crudely, Indians produced furs, while Métis and Europeans traded for them.

Reductions in the size of the workforce also led to major changes in its composition. Prior to 1821 the officers of the Hudson's Bay Company tended to be English or Orkneymen, while company servants were predominately from the Orkneys. The company had begun hiring some children of

A Métis encampment on the plains, by Paul Kane. The painting suggests the scale of Métis buffalo hunting expeditions in the mid-19th century.

their own employees, but Métis or Mixed Blood employees remained relatively rare. The North West Company drew most of its officers from Scotland, although not the Orkneys, and from Upper and Lower Canada. A significant proportion of the leading wintering partners were actually the descendants of Loyalists who had settled in Upper and Lower Canada after 1783. The NWC recruited most of its canoemen, labourers, and tradesmen in the Canadas, although some children of company employees did follow their fathers into work in the fur trade prior to 1821. The NWC also offered more opportunities for Mixed Blood and Métis children to find work as suppliers of provisions — including buffalo meat and pemmican — and as temporary employees at posts.

After 1821, this situation changed. Reductions in the number of full-time jobs with the new Hudson's Bay Company meant expansion of part-time labour at posts. With smaller staffs, posts increasingly turned to local Métis groups

and First Nations as sources of temporary or part-time labour. For example, at York Factory, many local residents found work loading and unloading cargo when the annual supply ship arrived from Britain, or worked in the summers on the boat brigades. Others worked as hunters or fishers, supplying post residents with fresh game and fish, which in turn cut down on the need for expensive imports of food from Britain at all posts.

Métis and Mixed Blood people filled a higher and higher proportion of the remaining full-time jobs with the Hudson's Bay Company. In the Northern Department of the HBC, the number of employees hired from the Canadas dropped sharply — more proof that William McGillivray's comment about the fur trade being lost to Canada was prophetic. In 1830 over 40 percent of the HBC servants came from the Canadas. This number dropped to just over 20 percent in 1840, and about 17 percent in 1850. By 1870 the number was under five percent. During the same period, the proportion of servants hired from Scotland, including the Orkneys, Lewis, Shetland, and the Highlands, actually increased slightly from about 30 percent in 1830 to 40 percent in 1870.

The startling change, however, was among those listed as "native," meaning native to the North West, in company employment records. In 1830, about 25 percent of the servants of the Hudson's Bay Company were listed as "native." By 1850, they were the largest single group of servants, at

Photograph of Ojibwa canoe and women on Albany River, Ontario, circa 1907.

over 40 percent of the workforce, and from 1860 to 1880 they remained substantially more than 50 percent of the entire HBC workforce.

The numbers of Métis and Mixed Bloods also increased significantly among company officers, although this took some time to manifest itself at the highest ranks of commissioned officers. Because no commissioned officer could be appointed until a share was freed by the death or retirement of a previous chief factor or chief trader, and because commissioned officers were chosen from the ranks of senior clerks, it took a decade or more for even the most able, most ambi-

tious, and best connected of salaried officers to reach such an exalted rank. Nevertheless, by the 1850s, Mixed Blood–commissioned officers were increasingly common and often had charge of entire fur trade districts.

Most had fathers who had previously been senior company officers, and patterns of patronage and kinship are easily traced within the Hudson's Bay Company. Most of the "native" commissioned officers also had been given the kind of elite education that their fathers' wealth could buy. Many sons of senior company officers were sent to Britain or Canada to school, or to St. John's College in Red River, where they were taught Latin and Greek rather than how to prepare a moose hide. After years of such schooling, it is not clear just how "native" they would have considered themselves, and matters of social class undoubtedly took precedence over ancestry.

Nonetheless, the fur trade is unusual in the history of colonial trading enterprises in that it became demographically more and more self-sufficient, drawing its personnel from the very communities and families it created. It is also unusual because significant numbers of people with mixed European and Aboriginal ancestry rose to positions of genuine prominence in the trade. Arguably, by the 1840s and 1850s, the point made by Gerald Friesen about two parallel fur trades — one Euro-Canadian and the other Aboriginal — had mutated into something subtly different. During the period between 1821 and 1857, the palisades around fur trade posts no longer marked a clear cultural and demographic dividing line with Aboriginal people outside and Europeans inside.

This is not to say that the fur trade was an early example of multicultural diversity and tolerance. The Mixed Blood

Riel House, Winnipeg.

sons of company officers often experienced prejudice and many, along with their fathers, complained that the system of company hiring and promotion limited their opportunities. The views of sons of tradesmen and labourers are not so well documented, but they too no doubt endured the casual stereotyping and labelling common to the period. James Ross of Red River later asked the question, "What if mama were an Indian?" He clearly meant the question rhetorically and felt that it should matter not a jot. However, background did continue to matter in the fur trade, which was increasingly plain when looking at marriage and family patterns.

For years fur trade historians almost totally ignored the roles of women in the fur trade, as if somehow only men were involved in the story. Obviously this is not the case, and two pioneering books by historians Sylvia Van Kirk and Jennifer Brown have done a great deal to redress this oversight. Both make the point that women in the 18th and 19th centuries were involved in most aspects of fur trade history, and that marriage and family patterns reveal great deal about the fur trade as a social system as well as an economic one.

Van Kirk in particular based her analysis of fur traders' views on marriage on a comment made in 1840 by James Douglas to James Hargrave on the occasion of his marriage to a Scottish woman, Letitia Hargrave. Douglas suggests this marriage reflected a larger historical evolution:

> There is a strange revolution in the manners of the country; Indian wives were at one time the vogue, the half-breed supplanted these, and now we have the lovely tender exotic torn from its parent bed to pine and languish in the desert.

Ignoring the odd and somewhat sexist gardening metaphor, Douglas's comment suggests a relatively simple three-stage evolution of fur trade marriage from First Nations women, to Métis and Mixed Blood women, to European women.

Although things were more complex than this, Douglas's comment contains more than a grain of truth. Tradesmen and labourers working for the Hudson's Bay Company continued to marry Aboriginal women well into the 20th century. Few, if any, had much interest in "lovely tender exotics" and made more practical marriage choices of women who could make moccasins, trap and prepare furs, and handle living at a fur trade post. Some officers did decide to marry women from Britain or the Canadas. Many, however, saw the advantage of marrying the daughters of more senior officers or simply women who were comfortable living in fur trade communities in ways that Letitia Hargrave's letters to friends and family in Scotland reveal she never was.

Nevertheless, the decision of prominent Hudson's Bay Company officials — including James Hargrave, Donald Ross, John Clarke, Donald Mackenzie, James McMillan, John George McTavish, and, most notably, George Simpson — to marry European women suggests a growing belief among the elite of the fur trade that the answer to James Ross's question was it mattered a lot who your wife and the mother of your children was.

Francis Simpson.

Bastion at Fort Langley, British Columbia, circa 1862.

Many of the men who married European women did so after ending earlier relationships with Aboriginal women. George Simpson is a good example of this trend. Although few dared to question his actions, the behaviour of George Simpson has been seen by many as both particularly callous and revealing of changing social attitudes. Simpson had had several long-term relationships with women and had fathered at least four children in the North West between 1820 and 1829. In 1829 he returned to Britain on furlough in search of a wife, as did his close friend John George McTavish. Both were successful, and Simpson married his cousin Frances Simpson in 1830 before returning with her, first to Montreal and then Red River. Simpson made a point during their time in Red River of limiting Frances's exposure to any women he considered were not "respectable." This meant, in effect, that women who were not European, whatever the position of their husbands, were treated as somehow inferior.

As there were also missionaries in Red River after 1818, it was possible to marry under the auspices of a church and not just in "the custom of the country." This too served as a line of division between those who held that a man and woman who had lived together for years were married and their children completely legitimate and those who held that this

practice was immoral and socially intolerable. It is not an exaggeration to say that the issues of marriage and race undermined the harmony of post communities in Red River in the 1830s and 1840s, and by the 1850s, Chief Trader Robert Campbell felt it reasonable to conclude:

> It is too well known that few indeed of those joined to the ebony and half ebony damsels of the north are happy or anything like it; and few or none of them have pleasure, comfort or satisfaction of their Families.

How Campbell might claim to speak for so many is unclear, but the attitudes behind his comment made it something of a self-fulfilling prophecy.

Making the fur trade more self-sufficient had other impacts on Red River, which the Selkirk family had handed back to the Hudson's Bay Company to govern in 1836. Red River was originally conceived of as an agricultural outpost in the very heart of the North American continent, but this idea ignored the fact that there were few markets for the settlement's production other than the handful of missionaries who located there and the Hudson's Bay Company itself. Simpson and other senior HBC officials tried to encourage a number of enterprises in the colony that would provide an economic alternative, but efforts to develop a buffalo-wool company, sheep ranching, and a tallow business all failed.

Instead, Red River residents developed a range of economic strategies to support themselves. Most agriculture was for personal consumption, although the Hudson's Bay Company did purchase some excess production — especially food supplies. For example, at Lower Fort Garry, located just north of the main Red River settlement, the HBC baked biscuit using locally grown wheat, which was then shipped to posts through the North West. Similarly, flour sales to the company rose gradually from roughly 10 tonnes in 1825 to 50 tonnes in 1838. That year the HBC paid Red River wheat producers roughly £600 for their flour, although, spread across a population of several thousand people, this was not a huge sum. Red River also continued to produce large quantities of fresh and dried buffalo meat and pemmican, which were purchased by the HBC. Nevertheless, these economic opportunities were limited, and some residents of Red River and former company employees or their children decided to go into the fur trade on their own behalf as independent traders.

This activity can really be seen as a continuation of the long tradition of Aboriginal middleman traders. Métis and Mixed Blood people were ideally suited for this role as trade intermediaries. They often spoke multiple languages, including English, French, Cree, Chipewyan, and Blackfoot, for example. They usually had close personal and family ties to both the First Nations communities and Euro-Canadian fur traders, making them comfortable in both hunting camps and trading posts.

Initially, the Hudson's Bay Company had little concern with this private trade and even gave it some modest encour-

agement. Essentially, Métis traders were trading *en derouine:* taking trade goods acquired from the HBC posts out to Aboriginal camps and purchasing furs that in turn got traded at the HBC posts. Métis traders collected and transported furs to company posts and thus provided a service to both producers of those furs and the HBC as their purchaser. So long as the HBC was really the only source of trade goods and the only market for furs, private trade benefited both parties, and the company made few efforts to prevent it.

This laissez-faire attitude, however, began to be strained in the 1830s and early 1840s, as private traders found alternatives to trading their furs back to the Hudson's Bay Company. American fur trade companies were well established on the Missouri River as far west as what is now Montana by the early 1830s, and a trickle of furs began to escape along the

Painting of Fort Vancouver, 1845.

southern margins of the HBC trade empire. This trade leakage gradually increased as settlements such as St. Paul in Minnesota were established, and soon it became a direct threat to the HBC. In 1844, Norman Kittson of the American Fur Company built a post at Pembina that was easily reached by independent traders from Red River, and he began trading in direct competition with the HBC. That same year, the Crow Wing Trail, linking settlements in Minnesota with Red River, was also opened.

The Hudson's Bay Company tried to respond by instituting a system to license traders, but Métis and Mixed Blood leaders opposed this attempt to assert monopoly trade rights. the HBC countered by invoking its charter and the trade privileges granted in 1821 by the British Parliament to the merged company. Nothing came immediately of this debate, but it foreshadowed important battles to come.

It was not just in Red River, however, that troubles arose in 1844, and the period A.S. Morton described as "profound quiet and … extraordinarily successful fur trade," was ending.

Far to the west, the Hudson's Bay Company had acquired through the North West Company a significant network of trading posts west of the Rockies along the Pacific coast. Their distance from York Factory made them hard to supply, although George Simpson encouraged a number of different approaches to the problem. In particular, he briefly thought that pack horses sent from Fort Edmonton to the Jasper House area could then transport trade goods through the adjacent Athabasca Pass and Yellowhead Pass to the Columbia and New Caledonia districts respectively. Although brigades did use these and other mountain passes on occasion, it was soon realized that the Pacific coast fur trade really had to be supplied by ships sailing around Cape Horn to Fort Vancouver (built near the mouth of the Columbia River in 1825) and Fort Langley (built on the Fraser River in 1827). These two main posts would act as the main administrative and supply centres for smaller inland posts.

The Hudson's Bay Company dominated the fur trade from the Columbia River north because of its size and superior financial resources, but it was always understood that the trade in this entire region was open to British and American interests. Trade on the Pacific coast was governed by a separate set of international agreements that dated back to the Nootka Sound Convention of 1790. In 1818 the United States and Britain agreed to the Anglo-American Convention that proposed joint occupation of the area from California, which was still part of Mexico, north to what is now Alaska. This agreement was renewed in 1827, but it was never intended to be a permanent solution for governing the area.

In the early 1840s, the idea of joint occupancy came under attack, largely because of increased American settlement in the region via the famous Oregon Trail. American settlement increased south of the Columbia River, and settling the boundary became a major political issue in the 1844 presidential election. James Polk campaigned on the slogan "Fifty-four Forty or Fight" — a proposition that would have extended American territory well north of the 49th parallel and taken in most of modern British Columbia. When Polk was elected president, the Anglo-American Convention was doomed.

Negotiations for a division of the territory were quickly begun. Britain, at the behest of the Hudson's Bay Company and based in large part on claims to trade in the area dating back to David Thompson's Columbia venture of 1811, argued for a border that followed the Columbia River. The Americans disagreed. In the end, the more extreme claims of all parties were rejected, and it was decided simply to extend the border of the 49th parallel west to the Pacific coast. The HBC did manage to secure one major concession: all of Vancouver Island, including its valuable property around Fort Victoria, would remain British, even though much of the southern part of the island lay below the 49th parallel. The agreement, which was formalized as the Oregon Treaty of 1846, represented a compromise satisfactory to all parties, although the HBC did have to abandon valuable posts and a significant volume of trade to the Americans.

Simpson, ever the opportunist, tried to turn the Oregon Crisis to the advantage of the Hudson's Bay Company in other areas. He lobbied the British government to send troops to Red River to protect the settlement and the fur trade, should "Fifty-four Forty or Fight" turn out to be a promise rather than just political rhetoric. Britain agreed, and in 1846 three companies of the Sixth Regiment of Foot, a total of 347 officers and men, were dispatched to Red River.

In addition to providing a welcome economic boost to the

settlement and its main merchant, the Hudson's Bay Company, the soldiers also helped support the HBC's government of Red River. Emboldened by this military support, local the HBC officials tried again to suppress the independent traders from Red River and the growing trade with Pembina and St. Paul. Métis and Mixed Blood free traders countered by trying to convince the British Colonial Office to revoke the HBC's official trade monopoly.

So long as the troops remained in Red River, the dispute simmered, but with the Oregon issue settled, the Sixth Regiment was withdrawn in 1848. Simpson and Hudson's Bay Company officials in London argued for a replacement, but all that was offered was a small detachment of semi-retired soldiers, the Chelsea Pensioners. The Pensioners were hardly sufficient to cow the Red River free traders, but Chief Factor John Ballenden, the officer in charge of Red River, decided to press the issue.

On Ballenden's orders, four Red River free traders were arrested in 1849 for trading furs with Indians. The Red River Métis and Mixed Blood communities were united in absolute opposition to the arrest. Waves of protest swept through the settlement, since most Red River residents traded on occasion, and without some access to private trade, the settlement had very shaky economic prospects. A committee was formed to help defend the accused. One of its leading members was Louis Riel, the father of the more renowned Louis Riel who rose to prominence defending Métis rights in 1870 and 1885.

The first of the accused to be brought to trial was Guillaume Sayer. Armed Métis surrounded the court, and James Sinclair, a leader of the Métis and Mixed Blood communities, offered to act as Sayer's legal counsel. Finally a jury was found, though most had little desire to hear such a case, and the trial took place. The jury, after some deliberation, actually found Sayer guilty of trading illegally but recommended mercy, as Sayer and other Métis free traders honestly believed they had a right to trade on their own behalf. Ballenden considered that he had proved his legal point and Sayer was not sentenced. Ballenden also withdrew all other charges against Sayer and his fellow accused.

When the result was announced, the response was not exactly what Ballenden and the Hudson's Bay Company had hoped for. The armed Métis surrounding the court took the

verdict and lack of sentence to mean that Sayer was found innocent and supposedly left shouting, "La traite est libre" [The trade is free]. The HBC gave up the struggle and, from 1849 on, Red River Métis and Mixed Bloods traded openly with American fur companies at Pembina and St. Paul.

As historian W. L. Morton has commented, the Sayer Trial and the precedent it set — allowing private trade in spite of the theoretical existence of an the HBC trade monopoly — "marked the beginning of the end of the old order" in the North West. The full implications of the change would not become clear for nearly a decade, but Red River, the fur trade, and the Hudson's Bay Company all would never quite be the same again.

A re-enactor at Lower Fort Garry.

8

THE FUR TRADE IN A CLIMATE OF CHANGE, 1850–1883

Throughout most of what is now Canada, the actual process of trading furs continued largely unchanged from decade to decade until the late 1840s, despite companies being formed and merged, changes in the language of trade, and even new developments in technology and fashion. For example, after 1839, silk increasingly replaced beaver fur as the preferred material for hat making. The change did not take place overnight, but gradually demand for beaver did decline. Hatters bought beaver by weight rather than as pelts and, after almost two centuries, the Hudson's Bay Company finally stopped offering beaver fur for sale by weight in 1859.

Of course, the Hudson's Bay Company had long since stopped relying on hat makers for its profits, but the substitution of silk for beaver felt and the end to selling beaver by the pound can be seen as symbolic of much more profound changes in the fur trade after 1850. Irene Spry has described the period from 1857 to 1896 in the old fur trade the North West as the transition from a "nomadic" to a "settled" economy. Put another way, it was during this period that the North West split into a North and a West.

Still, changes would have been hard to notice initially — outside of Red River. At most other posts, Aboriginal groups living nearby might visit sev-eral times a year, but for the majority, who lived at some distance, the usual practice was to come in to trade twice a year at most. In the autumn, bands would arrive to trade for the supplies they needed for winter hunting and trapping. The Hudson's Bay Company would advance these supplies on credit, based in part on the knowledge the officer in charge of the post had of an individual's character and skill as a hunter and trapper. This "debt," as fur traders called it, was paid off — usually in full and with some extra margin for new supplies — when groups returned to the post in late spring or early summer with their winter hunts.

This system of barter trade required considerable trust on both sides. Aboriginal fur producers had to trust that the tedious work of catching and preparing furs and then transporting them to posts would be rewarded by finding the supplies they needed at a reasonable price. Fur traders had to rely on fur producers to return year after year to the same post and to pay off their debt with the produce of another season's labour. Examples can be found of occasions when this system failed: when fur traders tried to secure a higher profit by short-changing customers, by selling substandard goods, or by abandoning posts so that there was no one there to

Photograph of Peigan at Rocky Mountain House, 1871.

trade with when groups arrived. For example, a large party of Blackfoot arrived at Rocky Mountain House in 1861 and found the post closed. Apparently angered by this discovery after travelling several hundred kilometres to trade, they burned the post — a small reminder to the Hudson's Bay Company that trade imposes obligations on both parties.

Examples can also be found of Aboriginal producers who ran up huge debts or travelled from post to post or company to company to secure goods on credit that was never repaid. To a remarkable degree, however, both the purchasers and the producers of furs made the system work. Examples of outright fraud and unscrupulous dealings are relatively rare in fur trade records, although all parties bargained hard and tried to secure the best price and the best goods in trade.

The system also enabled buyers and sellers to adjust to unforeseen circumstances, such as variations in the populations of fur-bearing animals year by year. The debt or barter trade system allowed traders to extend additional credit one year with the expectation that it would be repaid a year or two later when trapping improved. This meant that producers did not absolutely have to produce a specific quantity of furs in any given year, which allowed some latitude in managing the game and fur resources in their hunting territories. Traditional hunting and trapping practices (such as varying the area selected for hunting from year to year and season to season) and cultural and spiritual prohibitions against certain hunting behaviours (such as killing all the beavers in a lodge or hunting certain animals at particular times) helped to keep animal populations at sustainable levels.

Aboriginal groups retained a fair degree of control over resources and their participation in the fur trade under such a system. The balance of power was not necessarily skewed in favour of fur trade companies. Unless you believe that Aboriginal peoples became dependent upon trade goods almost immediately, it seems fair to suggest that they chose to trade rather than acting under any form of coercion or compulsion.

By the mid-19th century, however, the situation was changing rapidly, and not to the advantage of most Aboriginal

A beaver skin.

peoples. Some historians suggest that the Hudson's Bay Company's trade monopoly was the key factor in this change, since it meant that the producers of furs no longer had any ability to play one set of traders off another. One argument against this view is that where competition did still exist, especially near the border with the United States and in eastern Canada on the fringes of settled agricultural areas, it is not clear that fur producers were obviously better served.

Increased competition for land and resources in the face of a growing agricultural population at Red River and elsewhere may have had an impact, as did industrialization. Harold Innis noted that fur traders in the 19th century were able to secure the benefit of cheaper trade goods and lower transportation costs without necessarily passing this advantage along to their customers in the form of either higher prices for furs or lower prices for trade goods. Other historians have emphasized the role of resource depletion in changing the relations of trade. When supplies of fur-bearing animals declined, the cost of acquiring furs rose, especially in terms of time and labour. It also could

Trade blankets, now often referred to as Hudson's Bay blankets, are still popular sales items — just as they were in the 18th and 19th centuries.

A 19th century painting of a buffalo dance, by George Catlin.

mean that Aboriginal fur producers had to divert more and more of their effort from subsistence hunting and other crucial activities to trapping and preparing furs for trade.

The question of the environmental and ecological impact of the fur trade remains a complicated and contentious one. For years historians and economists assumed that the fur trade led all but inevitably into resource depletion, and that this in turn was a major factor in driving fur trade companies to expand, whenever possible, into new areas. Literally putting a price on the head of every beaver, fisher, marten, and fox in a region, the fur trade increased the risk of over-exploitation of animal populations. Fur trade records are also filled with comments about declining numbers of specific animals, although these statistics may reflect normal fluctuations in animal populations as much as the effects of over-hunting. In some cases the comments may also be excuses offered by company officers for poor fur returns rather than strictly factual descriptions of the local situation. Certainly in many cases, local areas that were reputedly "trapped out" recovered nicely and produced good fur returns within a few years.

There is, however, good evidence to suggest that the fur trade really did have a significant impact on a variety of resources. The demand for timber for building and wood for stoves and fireplaces led to the cutting of forests for dozens of kilometres around some posts, especially those near the Hudson Bay, where large stands of forest were rare. By the mid-19th century, York Factory and Churchill were reduced to bringing in firewood and lumber over huge distances because any tree of any size near the post site had long since been cut down. In the Peace River district, the local herds of buffalo were gone by the early 1830s, apparent victims of a combination of disease, bad weather, and over-hunting for provisions. In the Oregon area in the 1820s and 1830s, the Hudson's Bay Company rather cynically outfitted trappers with the intent of trapping every possible fur-bearing animal in the Snake River area. They were ordered to "hunt as bare as possible all the Country South of the Columbia and west of the mountains." The idea was to wring the last possible advantage out of the area and thereby keep American traders out, even if it meant purposely ruining trapping there for years to come.

Fur trade companies consistently tried to encourage the view that fur and game resources should be open to exploitation by all, and the result was a classic example of what ecologist Garrett Hardin has termed "the tragedy of the commons." Hardin argues that land has a certain natural carrying capacity. In traditional societies, this maximum carrying capacity of the land for people and animals may not be reached because of factors such as war, disease, high mortality rates, technological limitations, and cultural inhibitions against over-consumption. However, as populations increase, certain tendencies appear. Individuals may be encouraged to appropriate more of any "open access," or common, resources for themselves and their families. Their rationale is that they will benefit personally from killing more beaver or buffalo, but the costs of that decision — declines in overall beaver or buffalo populations — are actually borne by all. If enough people come to this conclusion, the pace of over-exploitation quickens and soon a problem of declining resources can escalate into a crisis.

The usual response, aside from simply doing nothing and letting the whole situation collapse, is to try to limit access to these resources or to allocate their use by substituting a system of regulation or even declaring resources private or group property rather than treating them as a form of common property open to access by all. Both types of response appear in the 19th

Above: Voyageurs at Dawn, painted by Frances Anne Hopkins, 1871.
Below: A Hudson's Bay Company job posting.

WANTED.

A FEW stout and active **YOUNG MEN**, for the service of the **HUDSON's BAY COMPANY**, at their Factories and Settlements in AMERICA. The Wages to be given, will depend on the qualifications of each individual: very good hands may expect from £12. to £15. a year, besides a sufficient allowance of oatmeal, or other food equally good and wholesome. Each person must engage by contract for a period of **THREE YEARS**, at the end of which, he shall be brought home to Scotland, free of expence, unless he chuses to remain at the Settlements of the Company, where **THIRTY ACRES of GOOD LAND** will be granted, in *perpetual feu*, to every man who has conducted himself to the satisfaction of his employers. Those who are thus allowed to remain as settlers after the expiration of their service, may have their Families brought over to them by the Company at a moderate freight. Every man who chuses to make an allowance to his relations at home, may have any part of his wages regularly paid to them, *without charge or deduction*. No one will be hired, unless he can bring a satisfactory character for general good conduct, and particularly for honesty and sobriety; and unless he is also capable of enduring fatigue and hardship. Expert Boatmen will receive particular encouragement. Those who are desirous of engaging in this service, will please to specify their names, ages, and places of abode, as also their present station and employments, and may apply to

century fur trade, reflecting the widely held belief that beaver, buffalo, and other critical resources were in decline.

For example, after 1821, the Hudson's Bay Company tried several times to limit production of specific types of furs by trying to regulate sales. In restricting the purchase of furs such as beaver, the company hoped to nurse beaver populations back to more sustainable levels. This policy was also intended to keep fur prices in London high by restricting supply. Initially the company tried to limit purchases of beaver trapped during the summers, and in the 1830s it tried to set annual quotas on the number of beaver pelts it would purchase in each fur trade district.

These measures had limited success. Aboriginal trappers did not hunt beaver only for trade. Beavers were a significant food resource, and if the furs were not sellable to the Hudson's Bay Company, then they were still useful as clothing. Company officers also complained that refusing to trade certain furs alienated customers, and the HBC risked losing their trade altogether. By the 1840s, the company felt obliged to strengthen the policy. In 1841 the company directives noted "the impoverishment of the Country in the article of Beaver in increasing to such an extent" that an "immediate remedy" was needed. Officers at some 32 posts in both the Northern and Southern Departments were warned that if they did not reduce their purchases of beaver pelts to half the number of the pelts traded in 1839, they might be

Costumed guides at Victoria Settlement recreate life at a late 19th century post on the North Saskatchewan River. The post was built to serve a Metis community founded by a Methodist missionary, George McDougall, in 1863.

forced to resign from company service. They were told to use whatever means they had to reduce beaver hunting, and as an incentive they were allowed to give a 10 percent premium on other furs.

It was not, however, until 1844 that the numbers of beaver pelts traded began to decline noticeably. Nor did stocks of beaver increase everywhere. In fact, by the early 20th century, beaver had become rare enough that pioneer conservationists such as Grey Owl had to reintroduce beaver in several national parks.

By the 1840s and 1850s, some observers were also noting worrying changes in the numbers and range of buffalo herds. John Palliser, sent by the British government to report on the land and resources of the North West in 1857, wrote that the herds of buffalo were increasingly scarce, and he believed that those that remained were being forced northwards by American settlement, cattle ranching, and hunting for food and hides. This theory created an illusion that herd populations were not in decline, but Palliser and others believed the future of anyone relying on the buffalo hunt was bleak.

Métis and First Nations groups also knew something was amiss. Red River buffalo hunters had to travel farther and far-

ther south and west, towards the Cypress Hills and beyond, to find large herds, and access to them became a source of contention.

In 1851 the Red River Métis buffalo hunters fought a two-day battle with the Dakota near the Grand Coteau of the Missouri River, just southeast of what is now Minot, North Dakota. In 1856 American soldiers were sent to Pembina to prevent Red River hunters from crossing the border to hunt "American" buffalo.

Métis hunters from other areas also became involved in the buffalo trade. Large groups of Métis wintered on *hivernant* camps, which were established in the 1860s at Buffalo Lake and Tail Creek in what is now central Alberta. These camps drew together hundreds of people to winter on the plains and support themselves primarily through private trading and buffalo hunting. Other, more settled, communities also developed, such as the Victoria Settlement, a small but fascinating settlement of English-speaking Methodist Mixed Blood buffalo hunters established by Reverend George McDougall on the North Saskatchewan River in the early 1860s, and St. Albert and Lac Ste. Anne, Catholic Métis communities located near Fort Edmonton.

As Métis, Dakota, Blackfoot, Plains Cree, and others contended for the remaining buffalo, the number killed actually rose according to trade records and contemporary observers such as Palliser — just as Garrett Hardin's theory would predict. Demand for robes and hides increased sharply, particularly in the United States, and steamboats and railways made it possible to move such bulky items to market at a reasonable cost. As a result, the buffalo-robe and -hide market flourished just as the herds themselves went into an irreversible decline.

Given the risk of confrontation with Dakota or other

Plains First Nations over buffalo, the Red River Métis organized their hunt much like a military expedition. In fact, the hunt itself became the basis for a parallel system of government among the Red River Métis that was quite separate from the Hudson's Bay Company's "official" government. The Red River Métis organized two hunts every year. The fall hunt drew fewer people and was less intense because it was intended to produce hides, robes, and fresh meat rather than pemmican. The spring hunt was the more important, as it was intended to produce pemmican as well as hides and robes for trade. It usually began in early June and drew participants from across Red River. French-speaking Métis and English-speaking Mixed Bloods, along with their families, left Red River and travelled by cart to the Pembina Hills. There they congregated before setting off together to find the herds. Before the hunt left, a "president," or leader, of the hunt was chosen along with 12 "councillors" and other officials. Each group of 10 hunters, usually friends and relatives, also selected a "captain" to lead their particular group.

Rules for the hunt were drawn up by the president and councillors and carefully enforced by the captains. Most were designed to ensure that the hunt as a whole was successful and to prevent individuals or small groups from starting to kill buf-

Head-Smashed-In Buffalo Jump tells the story of buffalo hunting on the Canadian plains from the pre-contact period to the collapse of the buffalo herds in the 19th century.

falo and thus frightening off the herd before the general hunt could begin. Once again, these regulations represent a clear attempt to manage a common resource for the benefit of hunt members as a whole. At the same time, these hunts, with their near military organization, were equally intended to ensure that the Métis secured access to the remaining buffalo herds in the face of competing claims to the resource from Cree, Assiniboine, Dakota, Blackfoot, and other Plains First Nations.

Paralleling issues of resource depletion and trade relations, in the 1850s, the outside world began to take a greater interest in the old fur trade territories. Historian W. L. Morton claimed that up to 1849 most change in the North West really came from within, but after 1849 external events became more and more important.

American settlement in Minnesota and later the

This painting by Paul Kane gives a sense of the excitement — and danger — involved in "running" buffalo.

The view from the edge of the jump at Head-Smashed-In. The jump itself was only a small part of a massive system for hunting buffalo that included a gathering basin, kilometres of drive lanes, and butchering, processing and camping areas near the base of the jump.

Dakotas brought the threat of American expansion close to the old fur trade North West along with expanded opportunities for trade and new transportation options. The Hudson's Bay Company no longer had to rely on shipping trade goods in and furs out through York Factory. St. Paul could be reached by a combination of railways and steamboats, and from there, cart brigades could transport goods to Red River for redistribution across the North West. The HBC began experimenting with this new transport system in the 1858, and in 1859 American entrepreneurs succeeded in launching a steamboat, the *Anson Northup,* on the Red River itself. York Factory, like Fort William before it, began a swift decline as more and more of the HBC's trade was channelled through Red River. By 1872, York Factory was effectively abandoned as the main warehouse and distribution centre for the HBC. During the same period, the administrative centre of the company's trade shifted to Red River and Upper Fort Garry.

As American interest in Red River and the North West grew, so too did interest in the Canadas. After over three decades of ignoring the North West and the fur trade, Upper Canadian politicians in particular began to argue that the North West properly belonged to Canada, and that it could serve as a vast reserve of land and resources for a second

transcontinental nation in North America. Britain took a greater interest in this vast, but largely unknown, chunk of imperial real estate in the 1850s, prodded in part by the Oregon Crisis and the need to reconsider the trade concessions granted to the new Hudson's Bay Company in 1821.

The agreement to amalgamate the North West Company and the Hudson's Bay Company had come with a legal and political dowry from the British Parliament. The new company had been granted an exclusive licence for trade for a period of 21 years, not just in the area covered by the original the HBC Charter of 1670, but for the Athabasca, Mackenzie, New Caledonia, and Columbia districts as well. This trade licence was renewed early and with virtually no discussion for a further 21 years in 1838. However, the Sayer Trial had shown that the HBC trade monopoly was something of a legal fiction, and the licence was up for renegotiation in 1859.

Between 1838 and the late 1850s, the political landscape in Britain shifted. Britain had adopted a free-market approach to economics, exemplified by the passage of a new Corn Law in 1846 that reduced tariffs on imported grains to insignificant levels. In the political climate of the times, monopolies and exclusive trade privileges were not popular. A British Select Committee of the House of Commons was formed in 1857 to hear testimony on the conduct of the fur trade as part of a larger process of determining whether or not the Hudson's Bay Company should be given a further extension of its trade licence.

Two scientific surveys of the North West parallelled the Parliamentary inquiry. Both had similar objects and were charged with surveying the resources of the territories administered by the Hudson's Bay Company. The idea was to determine the potential of the region for agricultural settlement and other development. One was mounted by the Canadas and was led by Henry Youle Hind, a professor from Trinity College in Toronto. The second, and probably better known, expedition was organized by Britain and led by John Palliser.

Both expeditions were launched in 1857. Hind had completed his work by 1858, while Palliser and his companions continued their survey work until 1860. Both expeditions published substantial reports; in fact, Palliser and his associates published a variety of works. Both Hind and Palliser commented on the declining prospects of the fur trade and reported favourably on the agricultural and settlement prospects of the region. Palliser famously noted that the southern plains — Palliser's Triangle — were arid, and thus had limited potential for settlement. However, overall he felt that areas such as the Saskatchewan and Red River Valleys were suited to agriculture. Hind was even more optimistic. He wrote:

> It is a physical reality of the highest importance to the interests of British North America that this continuous belt can be settled and cultivated from a few miles east of the Lake of the Woods to the passes of the Rocky Mountains, and any line of communication, whether by waggon [*sic*] road or railroad passing through it, will eventually enjoy the great advantage of being fed by an agricultural population from one extremity to the other.

Taken together, the two expeditions exemplify the growing interest of the outside world in the Hudson's Bay Company's territories, and they provided a wealth of scientific knowledge on a region that was still largely unknown to outsiders. Moreover, both Hind and Palliser clearly believed that the future of the region did not lie in beaver pelts and muskrat skins.

The Select Committee covered similar ground. It looked into how the Hudson's Bay Company managed the fur trade and its relationship with missionaries, Aboriginal peoples, and its own employees. It also spent considerable time trying to determine whether or not the North West and the Pacific coast were suitable for large-scale agricultural settlement. Testimony collected by the Select Committee offers remarkable insight into the operations of the fur trade and the HBC in this transitional period.

George Simpson testified at length at the hearings and offered the official Hudson's Bay Company posi-

tion on the matters under consideration. Predictably, Simpson argued that the North West as a whole was unfit for settlement — at least outside of Red River and a handful of other specific locations — and that the trade rights granted to the HBC were necessary and should be extended. Simpson pointed to what he considered to be numerous achievements of the company, such as limiting the use of alcohol as a trade good, encouraging missionary activity and education, developing a legal system, and the distributing land in Red River on very favourable terms.

The transcript of the hearings, however, makes it clear that Simpson's testimony was not particularly well received. He had earlier claimed in print that the entire region from the Lake of the Woods to the Rockies was highly fertile, and Committee members returned again and again to this point. Most thought that the interests of a fur trade company did not genuinely include encouragement of settlement. Edward Ellice, whose connection with the fur trade dated back to the North West Company, testified that the fur trade was really not profitable outside of the far north. He claimed that the Hudson's Bay Company barely broke even on trade on the Saskatchewan and lost money in any area near the American border from the Great Lakes to the Pacific. He suggested that the HBC would be "glad" to surrender territory "for the purpose of settlement" to the Canadas, assuming that the new

HBC train laden with furs arriving at Calgary from the north, early 20th century.

owners provided for the costs of policing and government and made some effort to limit trade competition.

The inquiry was really Simpson's last hurrah as governor of the Hudson's Bay Company. He died in Lachine in 1860, not long after the Select Committee had decided to accept just a portion of Simpson's case. The majority report of the Committee did find that the HBC's "License for Exclusive Trade" should be extended, but only in the northern boreal forest regions where significant agricultural settlement was unlikely. The committee also suggested that Vancouver Island be turned into a separate crown colony, and that considera-

A drawing of Fort Edmonton on the North Saskatchewan River, Alberta, 1865.

tion be given to encouraging settlement of the Red and Saskatchewan River Valleys, as both Hind and Palliser had argued. In addition, the report noted that the way to achieve this goal was by transferring ownership and control of all areas suited to settlement from the to the Canadas.

Even this modest victory on trade rights was snatched away, however. The British government decided that the legal status of the Hudson's Bay Company charter was unclear and that without a judicial ruling on its meaning and validity, a new licence for exclusive trade could be offered for only one year. The HBC refused the proposal, and in 1859 the HBC trade monopoly lapsed. Of course, as A. S. Morton noted, the HBC had no real rival for the fur trade in British North

America in 1859, so the grant of such a short-term licence meant little anyhow.

Still, these events signalled significant changes in the fur trade. E. E. Rich, a noted historian of the Hudson's Bay Company, summarized those implications bluntly. He wrote that from 1859 to 1870, the political debate was over "territorial rights, not trading capacity." He also stated that after 1857, "the fur-trader as such became relatively unimportant." This may overstate the case somewhat, as the fur trade did not disappear — reports of its death have been consistently exaggerated — but political events in both Britain and the Canadas between 1857 and 1869 drew a clear distinction between a fur trade North and an emerging agricultural West.

This was really a bleak period for the Hudson's Bay Company. Simpson's death was followed by more corporate turmoil. Several prominent British and Canadian investors tried to develop a telegraph and transportation company to cross the Prairies. When the HBC refused to assist, a shadowy investment company with links to some of the most powerful business figures in Britain, the International Finance Association, bought control of the HBC in 1863. The appeal was not the fur trade business of the old company, but the potential value of its charter and land interests. The price was a relatively modest £1,500,000.

The International Finance Association produced a prospectus for potential investors, proposing development of a telegraph and postal system linking the Canadas with British Columbia, but the real negotiations began shortly after Nova Scotia, New Brunswick, and the Canadas formed a new nation, the Dominion of Canada, in 1867. One of the first acts of the government of the new federation was to begin discussions over the possible surrender of the Hudson's Bay Company's territory to Canada. The territory in question was enormous, stretching from Labrador to the Rockies, and setting a price for such an exchange was not simple. The negotiations were no secret as they dragged on into 1869. Astonishingly, no one seems to have considered the fact that this real estate deal also affected the lives of thousands of Indians and Métis. People in Red River felt particularly aggrieved that a sale of their community would occur without any consultation with them.

In the end, Canada settled on a final price, and the charter turned out to be worth a significant sum. King Charles's gift turned out to be a very lucrative one for investors in the International Finance Association. The company received a direct payment of £300,000 — a figure worth the equivalent of about £15,000,000, or CND $34,500,000, in 2002 figures — and grants of land amounting to roughly 7,000,000 acres. The Hudson's Bay Company received much more initial compensation for the surrender of its charter rights than Aboriginal peoples did for their supposed land surrenders under treaties.

The conclusion of the deal had to wait, however, until 1870, because the residents of Red River, led by Louis Riel, organized an effective resistance to the land transfer to Canada. The resistance was rooted in the social, economic, and political legacy of the fur trade, but the Hudson's Bay Company played little part in the unfolding story — further proof that the company and the fur trade were no longer central to the future of the much-discussed "fertile belt."

The incorporation of the North West into Canada did have almost immediate implications for the fur trade. The expansion of American trading posts along the upper Missouri River meant a growing American trade presence on the southern Canadian plains. American traders expanded outwards, particularly from Fort Benton on the Missouri River, and established a number of so-called "whiskey" posts north of the border in the 1860s. Fort Whoop-Up at Lethbridge and Spitzee Post near High River, Alberta, are good examples of whiskey posts. The trade at these posts was largely in buffalo hides, robes, and wolf skins. Whiskey — in reality, rather horrifying mixtures of alcohol, ginger, peppers, tobacco, and other additives to give the drink more bite — was a major trade item, but these posts supplied a range of more conventional trade goods as well.

Trade at whiskey posts was colourful, but also violent and dangerous to buyer and seller alike. For example, the infamous Cypress Hills Massacre of 1873 occurred when a dispute over missing horses arose between a party of

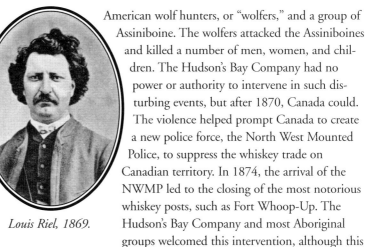

Louis Riel, 1869.

American wolf hunters, or "wolfers," and a group of Assiniboine. The wolfers attacked the Assiniboines and killed a number of men, women, and children. The Hudson's Bay Company had no power or authority to intervene in such disturbing events, but after 1870, Canada could. The violence helped prompt Canada to create a new police force, the North West Mounted Police, to suppress the whiskey trade on Canadian territory. In 1874, the arrival of the NWMP led to the closing of the most notorious whiskey posts, such as Fort Whoop-Up. The Hudson's Bay Company and most Aboriginal groups welcomed this intervention, although this

The fathers of Confederation in 1864.

trade was living on borrowed time anyhow. By the late 1870s, there were no free-ranging buffalo herds left in Canada to support a hide, robe, or pemmican trade — or the Aboriginal peoples of the plains region.

Twenty years earlier, this lack would have been a disaster for the Hudson's Bay Company, which had relied on steady supplies of buffalo meat for post provisions and pemmican for its boat brigades. The HBC trading posts in Red River and along the Saskatchewan River system as far west as Rocky Mountain House were built and maintained as sources of food as much as fur. However, the economic and technological changes of the 1860s and 1870s had all but eliminated the need to maintain posts outside the boreal forest. Abandoning York Factory as a transhipment point in favour of moving trade goods and furs via Red River and St. Paul by cart, steamboat, and railway meant that the system of York-boat brigades fell into decline. It also meant that beef, flour, and other food supplies could be purchased at Red River from the growing agricultural population of the Canadian west, or imported at much lower cost than before.

The Hudson's Bay Company responded by largely abandoning the fur trade in the plains and parklands areas. This does not mean that furs were never traded there after the 1870s, but increasingly the HBC closed trading posts as areas opened for settlement — for example, Rocky Mountain House was permanently closed in 1875 and Fort Carlton in 1885. In Winnipeg, Edmonton, Calgary, and other growing settlements, the company transformed itself into a retail sales operation instead. Company personnel records underline this story of retreat and retrenchment. The Northern Department of the HBC employed 585 servants in 1870, but just 270 in 1880, and 202 in 1885.

Most general Canadian histories scarcely mention the fur trade after 1870. Like E. E. Rich, they assume that fur traders

After Alberta became a province in 1905, the last Fort Edmonton site was chosen as the location for the new provincial legislature. This 1915 photograph showing the old fort being demolished to make way for the new legislature building.

had played their part and were no longer crucial to Canadian history. Even fur trade historians see the period after 1870 as marked by decline and major change. Sylvia Van Kirk, for example, has written eloquently about what this change meant in human terms. She notes:

> In the post-1870 Canadian West, the goal, largely of settlers from Ontario, was to establish a modern, agrarian, British society. In this scheme of things, there would be little basis for the continuation of the economic and social exchange between white and native peoples that had been the foundation of the fur trade…. As the tenets of British culture gained hold in the west, the traditions and practices of fur trade society were demeaned and forgotten.

She describes the result as "a world we have lost" and suggests that Canada is the worse for it, since "the blending of European and Indian culture" that marked the fur trade "could have been an enriching human experience."

Such bleak evaluations of the state of the fur trade and its place in Canadian history are not wrong, but they obscure the fact that the fur trade was not totally "lost" in the 1870s and 1880s. It was more in the process of relocation due to profound political and economic changes.

The completion of the Canadian Pacific Railway as a transcontinental transportation system in 1883 really marks the full entry of the plains and parkland regions of the Canadian west into a new regime. By 1883, resources of all kinds were treated as either private property or were open to access by all. The North West Mounted Police strictly enforced both approaches to resource management. Along with the major treaties, numbered 1 to 7 and signed between 1871 and 1877, this meant that with very limited exceptions, management of resources was transferred from Aboriginal peoples to the new Canadian state. The transition from a "nomadic" to a "settled" economy as described by Irene Spry was essentially complete — at least for the region between the 49th parallel and the Saskatchewan River system.

Epilogue

THE FUR TRADE IN A MODERNIZING WORLD, 1885–1945

If the arrival of the Canadian Pacific Railway in 1883 was an economic turning point for western Canada, the North West Rebellion of 1885 was a political one. The eventual defeat of Riel and his Métis supporters at Batoche cleared the way for wholesale settlement of the so-called "fertile belt." The Hudson's Bay Company anticipated these changes, and in 1884 it had reorganized itself yet again. The company established a subcommittee to oversee operations in Canada, and Joseph Wrigley was appointed as trade commissioner.

A pile of furs at Smith Landing, Fort Smith area, Northwest Territories, circa 1910.

The Canadian subcommittee foreshadowed the gradual metamorphosis of the Hudson's Bay Company from a British and London-based firm to the largely Canadian-based but essentially multinational company of the later 20th century. However, the appointment of Wrigley to manage company operations in Canada may be seen as even more symbolic. Unlike almost all previous senior HBC officials charged with managing company operations — even George Simpson spent a year apprenticing in the Athabasca district — Wrigley was not an experienced fur trader. His prior business experience was in the woollens industry, and historians such as Arthur Ray have suggested that in choosing Wrigley, the

HBC was signalling a clear shift in business emphasis away from the fur trade and into retail sales and other enterprises.

This change in business emphasis can also be traced in fur returns and where furs were traded. In the 1870–71 trading season, muskrat, beaver, and marten made up the vast majority of the furs acquired by the Hudson's Bay Company. That year, the company still collected over 10,000 buffalo robes as well. By the late 1870s, buffalo robes no longer figured in company trade returns at all.

In 1870, furs were traded at posts stretching from the Gulf of St. Lawrence to the Arctic Ocean on the Mackenzie River, but Red River was still the largest producer of furs in terms of sheer volume. Moreover, neighbouring districts, such as Lac la Pluie, Swan River, and the Saskatchewan, all of which stretched along the America border from Lake Superior to the Rockies, remained major producers of pelts, especially muskrat.

By the late 1880s, the geographic focus of the fur trade changed significantly. In 1887, the bulk of the Hudson's Bay Company's trade in the Red River District actually took place in the saleshops at Portage la Prairie and Manitou Post in southern Manitoba. Both served agricultural communities.

Much smaller volumes of business at St. Peter's, Dog's Head, and Brokenhead Reserves represented the more traditional fur trade business. Overall, this business was nowhere near the size it had been in 1870, when the Red River District produced more furs than any other.

In fact, by 1890 there were very few true trading posts anywhere south of a line stretching from Lake of the Woods across what is now southern Manitoba and central Saskatchewan, and then along the North Saskatchewan River to the Rockies. Fur producers did, on occasion, bring furs to Winnipeg or Edmonton to trade, but south of this line the

Reconstruction of a trapper's cabin at the Manitoba Museum.

Hudson's Bay Company was really in the business of operating retail stores and fur warehouses, selling land, and managing a transportation network. After 1909, Fort Edmonton was dismantled and replaced by Alberta's new legislative assembly building, and in Winnipeg, Calgary, and other urban areas, trading posts were transformed into retail stores. Company retail stores and saleshops still sold point blankets and axes, but rarely in return for furs.

North of this line, the Hudson's Bay Company still traded furs — and in some quantity — although it enjoyed a trade monopoly only in the most remote districts of the Canadian Shield and on the fringes of the Arctic.

The volumes of muskrat traded increased sharply in the 1880s and 1890s before peaking in the early 1900s at about seven times the number of muskrat pelts traded in 1870. As a result, it is quite misleading to suggest, as many survey histor-

ies do, that the fur trade as a whole declined after 1870. Muskrat was, however, a relatively low-value fur used to make coat linings or inexpensive fur coats and other outerwear. Beaver, by contrast, declined steadily in volume of trade. Although this decline was balanced by sharply rising prices for beaver fur, by the 1890s it had slipped behind marten and mink in terms of numbers of pelts traded. At the time, mink was considered an inferior fur, and the fur trade of the 1880s and 1890s was characterized by the sale of increasing numbers of pelts, but pelts of lower quality and value. To improve the prices paid for low-value furs, many were dyed and then marketed under new names. Dyed muskrat, for example, was sold as Red River or Hudson Bay "seal," and even as imitation mink or sable.

The development of rail and steamboat transportation increased competition for furs, since independent traders could reach northern communities that previously had had to rely on the Hudson's Bay Company. Nonetheless, the sheer scale of the HBC operations, and its well-integrated transportation and purchasing system, ensured that the company continued to dominate the Canadian fur trade up to World War I.

The handful of historians who have studied the 20th century fur trade see World War I as a major turning point in the industry. Although prices for beaver remained high, declining wild populations meant that by the 1920s and 1930s, beaver had fallen to seventh place in terms of numbers of pelts traded in Canada, far behind lower-value furs such as muskrat, squirrel, and ermine. The long decline of beaver as a trade item that began in the 1840s was essentially complete.

The war also reshaped fur marketing. London auctions were cancelled in 1914 and the Hudson's Bay Company tried to get its employees to temporarily suspend purchases of furs. This action enabled private buyers to further encroach on the company's business and led directly to an increase in shipments to Canadian and American auction houses located in Montreal, Winnipeg, Edmonton, New York, and St. Louis. the HBC never fully recovered from the trade disruptions caused by World War I: after the war, London no longer dominated fur-auction sales.

In the field, the result of the war was a further retreat of trading operations northwards. For example, posts such as

Dunvegan on the Peace River closed in 1918 — 113 years after the post was first opened by Archibald Norman McLeod for the North West Company after years of declining sales. The clerk's house at Dunvegan became a post office and telephone exchange. Similar stories were repeated across Canada. After 1918, the Hudson's Bay Company's remaining posts were concentrated in areas such as the Mackenzie River, Hudson Bay, James Bay, northern Ontario, and Quebec and the western Arctic.

Company financial records also indicate that in all but the most remote of these areas, barter trade was increasingly giving way to cash sales. This shift was mainly prompted by small, independent traders who preferred not to have to ship large quantities of trade goods to remote posts to exchange for furs. They wanted to pay cash, not axes or rifles, for the furs they bought. Trappers then could use their cash to buy trade goods from the Hudson's Bay Company and other larger firms, such as Revillon Frères, the Northern Trading Company, and Lamson and Hubbard, which tried to provide some trade goods for sale. In some ways, cash sales benefited fur producers, but they also eroded the old trade relations that enabled the HBC to offer credit to trappers and encouraged a sense of mutual obligation between fur buyer and seller.

The Mackenzie River area offers a good example of the nature of the fur trade in northern Canada in the 1920s and 1930s. Independent traders could travel north from Edmonton to locations such as Fort McMurray with relative ease. In fact, Fort McMurray had a direct rail connection with Edmonton by 1921. From Fort McMurray, steamboats and other river transportation allowed traders to reach any com-

Inuit at Revillon Frères post in Hudson Bay area. Note the signpost in the Inuit language, photograph circa 1908-1914.

munity from Lake Athabasca to the Arctic Ocean. Arthur Ray has calculated that in 1922, the Hudson's Bay Company secured just over 40 percent of the fur trade on the Mackenzie River. Two large rivals, Lamson and Hubbard and the Northern Trading Company, shared about 25 percent of trade. The remaining business was divided among dozens of smaller independent traders, who often simply resold their furs to larger companies.

The Hudson's Bay Company tried to respond by offering more cash sales, better prices, and more locations. In particular, as the company expanded into the Arctic, more of its trade was focused on this last fur trade frontier by the mid-20th century. It also made good use of its size and financial resources. Throughout the 1920s and 1930s, the HBC tried to buy out its largest competitors or at least portions of their operations. This process culminated in the purchase of the HBC's largest rival, Revillon Frères, in 1936. As quickly as the HBC acquired these firms, however, new small — and not so small — traders emerged.

Fur trader Philip Godsell, in his memoirs of this period, wrote:

Photograph of trade canoes of Revillon Frères on the Nipigon Route, Ontario, circa 1907.

Gone are the days of the picturesque and pompous Chief Factors. No longer do cannons roar and flags unfurl in honour of visiting potentates of the fur Trade…The Fur Lords no longer rule the red Men.

It is not clear that fur lords ever ruled Aboriginal peoples, but Godsell's comment summarizes a general sense that, even in the Arctic where Godsell worked, the fur trade had changed in fundamental ways by World War II.

By the end of the war, the Hudson's Bay Company posts traded only a quarter of the furs produced in Canada. Increasingly, it was not Godsell's "picturesque and pompous Chief Factors" but others who purchased trapped furs. Also, since the 1940s, more and more of Canada's fur trade was based not on trapping wild furs, but on fur ranching or farming enterprises. Today, roughly half of all the furs produced in Canada are not wild, but raised commercially. Ranched furs also tend to be valued

Hudson's Bay Company sign.

more highly than wild furs, so that proportionately a larger share of revenue goes to commercial fur farmers than to trappers. As a result, much of the current industry is no longer focused on Aboriginal producers trading with companies such as the Hudson's Bay Company.

Since World War II, and especially in the last three decades, the fur trade has become increasingly political. Campaigns against inhumane trapping techniques, the rise of the animal rights movement, and environmental concerns have all had profound effects on the fur trade. Sales of some furs have almost completely collapsed, and there is no evidence that debates over the ethics of this ancient trade are likely to be resolved anytime soon.

Industry statistics suggest that the total value of the fur business in Canada may still be as high as $800,000,000 a year, although much of this total is based on manufacturing and retail figures. Nevertheless, the total sales of pelts in Canada in 2001 were valued at approximately $73,500,000. About one-third of this amount went to producers of wild furs, while ranched furs represent about two-thirds of this total. Thousands of Canadians still derive some portion of their incomes from the fur trade, although this number continues to decline, and fewer and fewer people can make trapping or trading a full-time occupation.

Harold Innis may overstate the case when he says that the fur trade "made" modern Canada, and Father Le Jeune's Innu friend may have been equally hyperbolic to say that the beaver "made" everything from guns to knives perfectly well. Still, the fur trade has been at the centre of Canadian history since the 16th century. There is no region of Canada the fur trade did not touch. It linked Aboriginal, French, British, and — later — other Euro-Canadian peoples in a shared enterprise. Its language and material culture represent a fascinating blending of Aboriginal and Euro-Canadian forms. It produced an enduring society and a distinctive people, Canada's Métis. To see the fur trade as "just a business" is not to see it at all.

A painting of voyageurs fixing their canoe at night, by Frances Anne Hopkins, 1871.

FURTHER READING

The enormous volume of material written on the history of the fur trade makes suggesting a handful of sources a daunting task. The following books and authors, however, are all worth reading.

The classic general history of the fur trade remains Harold Innis, *The Fur Trade in Canada: An Introduction to Canadian Economic History* (Toronto: University of Toronto Press, 1999). There are also several useful survey histories of the North West, including A. S. Morton, *History of the Canadian West to 1870–71* (Toronto: University of Toronto Press, 1973) and E. E. Rich, *The Fur Trade and the Northwest to 1857* (Toronto: McClelland & Stewart, 1967). The opening chapters of Gerald Friesen's, *Canadian Prairies: A History* (Toronto: University of Toronto Press, 1987) reflect more recent historical research and avoid some of the ethnocentrism of earlier fur trade scholarship.

J. M. Bumstead's, *Fur Trade Wars: The Founding of Western Canada* (Winnipeg: Great Plains Publications, 1999) gives a detailed account of the critical period from 1811 to 1821. W. J. Eccles, *The Canadian Frontier, 1534–1760* (Albuquerque: University of New Mexico Press, 1983) remains a good survey of the early Montreal-based fur trade of New France, and Arthur Ray's, *The Canadian Fur Trade in the Industrial Age* (Toronto: University of Toronto Press, 1990) is the most thorough study of the fur trade after 1870.

Two relatively new books offer good surveys of Aboriginal history in Canada: Olive Patricia Dickason, *Canada's First Nations: A History of Founding Peoples from Earliest Times* (Don Mills: Oxford University Press, 2002) and Arthur Ray, *I Have Lived Here Since the World Began: An Illustrated History of Canada's Native Peoples* (Toronto: Lester Publishing, 1996). Arthur Ray has also written several very valuable books on trade and trade relations. His *Indians in the Fur Trade: Their Role as Trappers, Hunters and Middlemen in the Lands Southwest of Hudson Bay, 1660–1870* (Toronto: University of Toronto Press, 1998) details the development of middleman trade systems in the fur trade and the role of Aboriginal groups in supplying posts with meat, fish, and other products. Sylvia Van Kirk's, *Many Tender Ties: Women in Fur-Trade Society, 1670–1870* (Winnipeg: Watson & Dwyer, 1999) and Jennifer Brown's, *Strangers in Blood: Fur Trade Company Families in Indian Country* (Vancouver: University of British Columbia Press, 1996) revolutionized fur trade studies by making it clear that women and families were also an integral part of the story. Métis history is also closely tied to fur trade history and is increasingly the subject of new research. A taste of some of this new work can be found in Theodore Binnema, Gerhard Ens, and R. C. Macleod (eds.), *From Rupert's Land to Canada* (Edmonton: University of Alberta Press, 2001) and Jennifer S. H. Brown and Jacqueline Peterson (eds.), *The New Peoples: Being and Becoming Métis in North America* (Winnipeg: University of Manitoba Press, 1985). Specific studies of individual First Nations and histories of particular fur trade posts, companies, and individual traders and explorers are easily found.

Associated Museums and Sites

Museums

Along with the Museum of Civilization in Gatineau, most of the large provincial and regional museums in Canada have displays and collections related to the fur trade. Local museums from Fort Chipewyan to Churchill also often have good fur trade exhibits and collections. Many American state and local museums also have large fur trade collections reflecting the continental reach of the trade. The following is just a small sample of potential sites to visit.

Canadian Museum of Civilization

100 Laurier Street, Gatineau, QC J8X 4H2
phone: 1-800-555-5621
Website: www.civilization.ca/cmc/cmce.asp
Canada's national museum has an outstanding collection of Aboriginal and fur trade materials. The Canada Hall exhibits feature several fur trade-related dioramas. The website is also worth exploring for fur trade-related material.

Centre d'interprétation de Place-Royale

27 Notre-Dame Street, Quebec, QC G1K 4E9
phone: (418) 646-3167
Website: www.museocapitale.qc.ca/019.htm
Part of the larger Canadian Museum of Civilization system, this interpretive centre depicts the founding of Quebec by Champlain and the early history of trade in the area.

Pointe-à-Callière Montreal Museum of Archaeology and History

350 Place Royale, corner of de la Commune, Old Montreal, QC H2Y 3Y5
phone: (514) 872-9150
Website: www.musee-pointe-a-calliere.qc.ca/indexan.html
This outstanding museum tells the story of the founding of Montreal and details the city's connection to the fur trade.

The Manitoba Museum

190 Rupert Avenue, Winnipeg, MB R3B 0N2
phone: (204) 956-2830
Website: www.manitobamuseum.ca
The Manitoba Museum has several excellent, permanent fur trade galleries. The *Nonsuch* and Hudson's Bay Collection galleries are particularly engaging.

Provincial Museum of Alberta

12845—102nd Avenue, Edmonton, AB T5N 0M6
phone: (780) 453-9100
website: www.pma.edmonton.ab.ca
The Syncrude Aboriginal Gallery is especially interesting for insight into the impact of the fur trade on Aboriginal peoples.

Prince of Wales Northern Heritage Centre

Yellowknife, Northwest Territories X1A 2l9
phone: (867) 873-7551
website: pwnhc.learnnet.nt.ca
An excellent museum and archives with displays that show the fur trade remains a significant aspect of life in the North.

Minnesota State Historical Society History Center Museum

345 W. Kellogg Boulevard. , St. Paul, Minnesota 55102-1906
phone: (651) 296-6126
Website: www.mnhs.org
The Minnesota State Historical Society operates a museum and a number of historic sites in Minnesota. Long active in fur trade studies, the Society's museum and archival collections have a strong fur trade focus, as do the historic sites operated by the Society.

The Museum of the Fur Trade

6321 Highway 20, Chadron, Nebraska 69337
phone: (308) 432-3843
Website: www.furtrade.org
An interesting museum located on the site of an 1837 American Fur Company post. This museum has played a central role in the development of fur trade scholarship in the United States.

The Lewis and Clark Historic Trail Interpretive Center

4201 Giant Springs Road, Great Falls, Montana 59403-1806
phone: (406) 727-8733
Website: www.fs.fed.us/r1/lewisclark/lcic/
This new interpretive centre is dedicated to the story of the Lewis and Clark expedition. This expedition had significant consequences for the fur trade in the United States and Canada and led to the separation of the old Oregon Territory in 1846.

Historic Sites

As with museums, historic sites with fur trade connections can be found in virtually all areas of Canada and in many parts of the United States. The American National Parks Service operates literally dozens of sites with strong fur trade connections. State and local historical societies also operate many sites.

Some selected fur trade historic sites in the United States include:

Fort Vancouver National Historic Site

612 E. Reserve Street, Vancouver, Washington 98661-3897
phone: (360) 696-7655
Website: www.nps.gov/fova/

Fort Union Trading Post National Historic Site
15550 Highway 1804, Williston, North Dakota 58801
phone: (701) 572-9083
Website: www.nps.gov/fous/

Voyageurs National Park
3131 Highway 53 South, International Falls, Minnesota 56649-8904
phone: (218) 283-9821
Website: www.nps.gov/voya/

Grand Portage National Monument
211 Mile Creek Road, Grand Portage, Minnesota 55605
Website: www.nps.gov/grpo/

Mackinac State Historical Parks
P.O. Box 873, Mackinaw City, MI 49701
phone: (231) 436-4100
Website: www.mackinacparks.com/
The Mackinac State Historic Parks system operates several excellent fur trade sites in Michigan in the historic Michilimackinac area. Colonial Michilimackinac and Fort Mackinac are important sites in understanding the development of the fur trade on the Great Lakes.

Some selected fur trade historic sites in Canada include:

Ste.-Croix Island International Historic Site
Access from Bayside, New Brunswick or Calais, Maine
Website: www.pc.gc.ca/lhn-nhs/nb/stcroix/

The Habitation at Port-Royal National Historic Site
P.O. Box 9, Annapolis Royal, NS B0S 1A0
phone: (902) 532-2898
Website: www.pc.gc.ca/lhn-nhs/ns/portroyal/

Poste de Traite [Trading Post] Chauvin
157, Bord de l'Eau, Tadoussac, QC G0T 2A0
phone: (418) 235-4446

Sainte-Marie among the Hurons
Highway 12 East, Midland, ON L4R 4K8
phone: (705) 526-7838
Website: www.saintemarieamongthehurons.on.ca

Cartier-Brébeuf National Historic Site
175 de l'Espinay Street, P.O. Box 2474, Quebec, QC G1K 7R3
phone: (418) 648-4038
Website: www.pc.gc.ca/lhn-nhs/qc/cartierbrebeuf/

The Fur Trade at Lachine National Historic Site
1255 Saint-Joseph Boulevard, Lachine Borough, Montreal, QC H8S 2M2
phone: (514) 637-7433

Website: www.pc.gc.ca/lhn-nhs/qc/lachine/

Fort St. Joseph National Historic Site
Box 220, 100 Saint-Louis Street, Richards Landing, ON P0R 1J0
phone: (705) 246-2664
Website: www.pc.gc.ca/lhn-nhs/on/stjoseph/

Hudson's Bay Company Staff House
Moose Factory, ON
Website: www.heritagefdn.on.ca/ and follow the links to buildings in northern Ontario.

Macdonell-Williamson House
North side of Highway 17, Pointe-Fortune
phone: (613) 632-6662
Website: www.heritagefdn.on.ca/ and follow the links to buildings in eastern Ontario. The home of retired NWC fur trader John Macdonell.

Bethune-Thompson House (Williamstown)
19730 John Street, Williamstown, ON
phone: (613) 347-7192
Website: www.heritagefdn.on.ca/ and follow the links to buildings in eastern Ontario. The home of David Thompson in his retirement.

Duff-Baby House (Windsor)
221 Mill Street, Windsor, ON
Windsor Community Museum to arrange visits
phone: (519) 253-1812
Website: www.heritagefdn.on.ca/ and follow the links to buildings in southwestern Ontario. The home of a member of the Baby family of fur traders and merchants.

Ermatinger House (Sault Ste. Marie)
831 Queen Street East, Sault Ste. Marie, ON
Phone: (705) 759-5443
The home of fur trader Charles Oakes Ermatinger and his Ojibwa wife, Mananowe, or Charlotte.

Fort Témiscamingue National Historic Site
834 Chemin Vieux-Fort, Duhamel-Ouest, QC J9V 1N7
phone: (819) 629-3222
Website: www. pc.gc.ca/lhn-nhs/qc/temiscamingue/

Prince of Wales Fort National Historic Site
Box 127, Churchill, MB, R0B 0E0
phone: (204) 675-8863
Website: www.pc.gc.ca/lhn-nhs/mb/prince/

York Factory National Historic Site
P.O. Box 127, Churchill, MB R0B 0E0
phone: (204) 675-8863
Website: www.pc.gc.ca/lhn-nhs/mb/yorkfactory/

Lower Fort Garry National Historic Site
5981 Highway 9, Selkirk, MB R1A 2A8
phone: 1-877-534-3678 (1-877-LFG-FORT)
Website: www.pc.gc.ca/lhn-nhs/mb/fortgarry/

The Forks National Historic Site
401—25 Forks Market Road, Winnipeg, MB R3C 4S8
phone: 1-888-748-2928
Website: www.pc.gc.ca/lhn-nhs/mb/forks/

Fort Edmonton Park
7000—143 Street, Edmonton, AB T5J 2R7
phone: (780) 496-8787
Website: www.edmonton.ca/ and follow the links to the Fort Edmonton Park page.

Fort George and Buckingham House
c/o 8820—112 Street, Edmonton, AB T6G 2P8
phone: (780) 724-2611
Website: www.cd.gov.ab.ca/enjoying_alberta/museums_historic_sites/
The actual site is located near Elk Point, Alberta.

Victoria Settlement
c/o 8820—112 Street, Edmonton, AB T6G 2P8
phone: (780) 656-2333
Website: www.cd.gov.ab.ca/enjoying_alberta/museums_historic_sites/
The actual site is located near Smoky Lake, Alberta.

Fort Dunvegan
c/o 8820—112 Street, Edmonton, AB T6G 2P8
phone: (780) 835-7150
Website: www.cd.gov.ab.ca/enjoying_alberta/museums_historic_sites/

The actual site is located near Fairview, Alberta.

Fort Whoop-Up
Indian Battle Park, Lethbridge, AB T1J 4A2
phone: (403) 329-044
Website: www.fortwhoopup.com

Rocky Mountain House National Historic Site
Site 127 Comp 6, RR 4, Rocky Mountain House, AB T4T 2A4
phone: (403) 845-2412
Website: www.pc.gc.ca/lhn-nhs/ab/rockymountain/

Fort St. James National Historic Site
P.O. Box 1148, Fort St. James, BC V0J 1P0
phone: (250) 996-7191
Website: www.pc.gc.ca/lhn-nhs/bc/stjames/

Fort Langley National Historic Site
P.O. Box 129, 23433 Mavis Avenue, Fort Langley, BC V1M 2R5
phone: (604) 513-4777
Website: www.pc.gc.ca/lhn-nhs/bc/langley/

Batoche National Historic Site
P.O. Box 999, Rosthern, SK S0K 3R0
phone: (306) 423-6227
Website: www.pc.gc.ca/lhn-nhs/sk/batoche/

Fort William Historical Park
Vickers Heights Post Office, Thunder Bay, ON P0T 2Z0
phone: (807) 473-2344
Website: www.fwhp.ca/homepage.html